Rachael McGill

THE LEMON PRINCESS

FROM AN ORIGINAL IDEA BY RUTH CARNEY

ADDITIONAL STAND UP COMEDY MATERIAL BY RICHARD STACEY

Thank you to Nia Gwynne, Joanna Marks, Simon Muller and Richard Stacey for their input to the script through workshop improvisations.

Thank you to Stephen Forber and Stephen Dealler for their invaluable input.

First published in 2005 by Oberon Books Ltd
521 Caledonian Road, London N7 9RH
Tel: 020 7607 3637 / Fax: 020 7607 3629
e-mail: oberonbooks@btconnect.com
www.bloomsbury.com

A catalogue record for this book is available from the British Library.

ISBN: 1 84002 542 5

Characters

MIKE CHAPMAN
40s, from Leeds

HEALTH MINISTER
40s, from the South of England

BECKY CHAPMAN
17, from Leeds

CHAIR OF THE INQUIRY
40s, from the South of England

KAREN RICHARDS
late 30s, from Leeds

KATIE CONWAY
reporter, 20s/30s, from London

CHARLOTTE (CHARLIE) CHAPMAN
9, from Leeds

DR CAROLINE HARDING
scientist, late 40s, from the South of England

DR ALAN ANDREWS
research scientist, 40s, from Leeds

PROFESSOR JACK LIEBERMANN
American research scientist, 50s, from New York

SCIENTIFIC EXPERT
American

NIGHTMARE DOCTOR 1
American

NIGHTMARE DOCTOR 2
American

*Five actors can play all the parts: Mike / Health Minister; Becky /
Chair; Karen / Katie / Nightmare Doctor 1; Charlie / Caroline /
Scientific Expert / Nightmare Doctor 2; Alan / Jack*

Main Action Settings, 1995–6

Leeds: Pub; pub dressing room; Mike's house (living room, Becky's room); Karen's house (living room); Alan's lab; hospital.

London: government office.

New York: press conference; hospital room; Jack's office.

Inquiry Setting, 1998

London: conference room

Staging

Movement between scenes is fluid, like a dance. Scenes should follow each other quickly, even overlapping. Transitions to and from the Inquiry should be marked through some non-naturalistic theatricality/music/lighting. When an actor has to change characters quickly this should be done with the minimum of props and costumes.

Note

'Prion' is pronounced 'pree-on' by the scientists, but Mike can pronounce it 'pry-on.'

ACT ONE

Scene 1

Pub. Recorded drum roll, voice over: 'Ladies and Gentlemen, a very warm welcome to the Playhouse Comedy Club. Put your hands together for your host for this evening, Mike Chapman!'

MIKE comes on. Recorded clapping.

MIKE: Thank you very much. How are we all this evening?

Improvised warm up, the weather, chatting to the audience.

Sir, where are you from? I'm sorry. No, I mean I'm sorry. How many married people have we got in tonight? They reckon married men with kids live longer. I reckon that's bollocks, it just seems longer. I should have known when I saw the mother-in-law. She's a cold woman, she wears fridge magnets for fucking jewellery. The last time some poor bastard got his hand in her knickers, he came out with a packet of frozen peas.

When I first met the missus I were a total innocent. Sixteen and I'd never even seen a naked flame. Things started badly. I wanted to keep our relationship pure before we got married so we never talked about sex or owt like that. But seeing her there in her little miniskirts and stilettos, I'd have these lustful thoughts and I'd get a hard on. It's terrible int it fellas? Especially on the bus. We'd be coming home from the pictures and she'd hold me hand and it'd just jump up. I were that embarrassed. Anyhow, she invited me home to meet her mother so I decided drastic action was necessary so I got some electrical tape and strapped me cock to me leg. I got to the door and knocked and her mother answered. I introduced meself and it were all going well and then the missus came to the top of the stairs naked shouting,

21

'Mam, have you seen me best bra and pants?' I took one look at her and kicked her mother in the face.

On our wedding night the wife says to me, 'Now that we're married, will you tell me what a penis is?' I said, 'Yes my love, I've been saving that special knowledge for our first night of conjugal pleasure and now I'll not only tell you what a penis is, I'll show you.' So I got it out and she says, 'Oh, it's like a cock, only smaller.'

Anyway, things have sorted themselves out now cause I've made a special purchase that'll solve all me problems. I've got a ferret. But this is no ordinary ferret. I got it off a bloke in the pub. He came in with this ferret in his pocket and I asked him what he was doing. He told me the ferret went everywhere with him cause it were specially trained to give amazing blow jobs and that he sold these ferrets for fifty quid each. I didn't believe it so he offered me a free, no obligation trial and put the ferret up me trouser leg. To cut a long story short, this ferret gave me the most fantastic blow job I've ever had and I gave the bloke fifty quid to send me one. Anyway, it arrived this morning and the wife unwrapped it and asked me what I were doing bringing vermin into the house. I told her it weren't vermin, it were a ferret and I'd paid fifty quid for it cause it gave wonderful blow jobs. She said, 'Well what do you expect me to do with it?' I said, 'Teach it to cook and then fuck off!'

He bows.

BECKY comes on, clapping.

MIKE puts his arm round her.

Thank you very much ladies and gentlemen. Now I'd like to introduce a cheeky little devil with a voice like an angel. My daughter Rebecca Chapman. And we're going to do a tune for you. Ready love?

BECKY: Yeah, Dad. I've been waiting half an hour for you to finish boring these people with stories about ferrets.

MIKE: That's my girl. She has great respect for my work actually.

BECKY: Yeah, if I can't get to sleep at night I just think of one of your gags. Works every time. Look, it's worked for that woman over there an' all.

MIKE: Nah, she int sleeping, she's kind of gazing at me dreamily. I get that a lot love. Don't tell your mother. See you in the bar after darling.

BECKY: I reckon you should stick to the day job, Dad. Oh, no, I forgot, you int very good at that either. If anyone here's been getting the wrong post it's cause me Dad's so hungover when he does his round he can't read the addresses...

MIKE: That's enough from you.

He starts the song. They sing 'Don't go breaking my heart', taking the male/female parts of the duet.

Scene 2

Dressing room. BECKY changing her shoes, doing her hair, MIKE having a fag.

MIKE: How about that lot eh? I thought we'd come into a morgue and were playing to a room full of stiffs.

BECKY: D'you see them two fat lasses right in the middle? Reckon they came to the wrong place, cause they do Weight Watchers in St Patrick's on a Friday.

MIKE: That were never two lasses, the dark one was a fella, he had a better tash than mine. Hurry up and we can get a pint in for the road.

BECKY: Nah, you go. I'm meeting Lyn. I'm going down Majestyks.

MIKE: You going out now?

BECKY: It don't start till eleven. Don't wait up.

MIKE: Don't get into no fights with them bouncers!

BECKY kisses him, exits.

Scene 3

ALAN's lab. ALAN enters with CAROLINE. The lab is messy.

CAROLINE: Oh. You tidied up for me.

ALAN: Yes. No, I really did.

She laughs.

I'll just show you the slides then we can go somewhere for lunch if you like.

CAROLINE: I'm fine. I only ever eat a salad at lunchtime these days. Tom likes to cook in the evening when he's home. Come on then, let's see your mouse brains.

They look at slides with a projector.

ALAN: So you can see the spongiform change…

CAROLINE: How long does it take to get to this stage?

ALAN: There's about eight months of incubation in mice before it gets to the brain. But once it's there it's like a chain reaction. This was two weeks on after no treatment.

CAROLINE: Gosh.

ALAN: And this one's after treatment with indomethacin.

CAROLINE: This is really impressive Alan.

ALAN: And this is with flupirtine. Not quite as spectacular but still.

CAROLINE: It's excellent.

ALAN: Yeah, they slow it down quite a lot. And the side effects aren't too bad so there's no reason they shouldn't prescribe them for CJD.

CAROLINE absently starts tidying up the lab, arranging piles of papers etc.

But I don't want to keep messing around with these old Alzheimer's drugs that slow it down. I need to be stopping it. And then getting the nerve cells to regenerate.

CAROLINE: That's a long way off. Isn't it?

ALAN: It's just a matter of getting drugs straight into the brain. I've been thinking about an intraventricular pump. Or trying to work out a peptidase inhibitor so I can use beta sheet breakers.

CAROLINE: No one's going to fund that sort of thing for CJD Alan. It's not Alzheimers is it?

ALAN: Maybe they will when they read what you've got to say.

CAROLINE: (*Excited.*) So what do you think?

ALAN: Sounds like you've got something.

CAROLINE: We need a much bigger sample before we can publish. And we're waiting for the neuropath. But I've got a feeling we might see something there that proves we're looking at a totally new variant of the disease…

ALAN: You've already got enough that proves that!

CAROLINE: We haven't Alan…

ALAN: Much younger age of onset than sporadic CJD, much longer duration of disease, totally different clinical course, different EEG…

CAROLINE: But it's only six cases. But if my feeling's right then the neuropath might show something that's nothing like sporadic CJD but is more like…

ALAN: Sheep scrapie.

CAROLINE: Exactly. Or BSE.

ALAN: I knew it. You've done it.

CAROLINE: Not yet. I'm months away and the funding's practically run out.

ALAN: But if you tell them what you've got so far they'll have to give you more funding. This could be really serious.

CAROLINE: I know. Maybe we should write to the Health Minister.

ALAN: Yes. Let's do it now.

He starts to type.

'Initial evidence suggests that animal TSEs can indeed jump the species barrier to humans.'

CAROLINE: Alan. This is the Health Minister remember.

ALAN: What?

CAROLINE: We have to start at the beginning.

She deletes what he's typed and replaces it.

'Creuzfeld Jacob Disease, or CJD, is a rare brain disease in humans for which there is no cure. The kind of disease it is is called a Spongiform Encephalopathy. Another example of this kind of disease is the one that cows get, which is called Bovine Spongiform Encephalopathy, or BSE.'

ALAN: 'We now suspect that a new variant of CJD unlike sporadic…'

CAROLINE: 'We now suspect that a new version of the human disease CJD might be emerging which is slightly different from the usual kind which only occurs by chance or genetic inheritance. This new version might have been transmitted…'

ALAN: No! 'might have been caught by people because they ate beef infected with BSE. We are concerned that potential exposure amongst the public…'

CAROLINE: 'We are concerned that there could be an epidemic.'

Scene 4

MIKE's house: KAREN, CHARLIE, MIKE.

MIKE: So we're going on like that, slagging off the audience and all sorts, and Becky goes out the dressing room and I'm having a little practice. (*Sings.*) 'Hey I'm gonna leave young thing alone, but ain't no sunshine when she's gone…' And Becky runs back in and she's gone like a beetroot all over and she goes Dad, we're never coming here again, we're f---ed. The dressing room mike's been on. They're all getting their drinks at the bar and then I heard you going, 'ain't no sunshine when she's gone' over the tannoy.

KAREN: No!

MIKE: I'm not joking. They heard all of it, Barry told me after.

CHARLIE: Dad, why were she like a beetroot?

27

MIKE: All red love.

KAREN: Was Barry mad?

MIKE: Nah, he pissed himself.

CHARLIE: Beetroot's purple Dad.

MIKE: All purple then love.

BECKY comes in wearing pyjamas.

Look at the state of you. What time did you get in?

BECKY: Hiya Auntie Karen. Get us a cup of tea Dad.

MIKE: Welcome to Mike's caff. Any other orders?

CHARLIE: Knickerbocker glory with chocolate sauce.

MIKE: You're getting as cheeky as your sister. Go and get dressed, we're taking your Auntie Karen to Morrisons.

CHARLIE: I don't wanna come to Morrisons.

KAREN: Hard cheddar cause you're coming.

CHARLIE: I wanna stay here with Becky.

BECKY: She can stay here Dad. I'm not doing owt.

MIKE: All right then, but I want you dressed Charlie.

CHARLIE: Becky int dressed.

MIKE: Now!

BECKY: We'll do princesses later Charlie.

CHARLIE: Cool.

CHARLIE exits

KAREN: Good night love?

BECKY: Yeah, wicked night. Ben were DJing, me and Lyndsay danced four hours solid.

MIKE: Ere, you weren't on that E were you?

BECKY: Dad! You know me. I don't need an E to get happy and trippy.

KAREN: So that Ben's your new bloke then is he?

BECKY: He's bent as a nine bob note.

MIKE: Int that always the way?

BECKY: Hey, that Marco were behind the bar though.

KAREN: He's all right.

MIKE: Yeah for you maybe. He's too old for her.

BECKY: He's only twenty-eight.

MIKE: Yeah, and you're only seventeen.

BECKY: He's cool.

MIKE: (*Foreign accent.*) 'ello Becky, would you like a nice big coke?

BECKY: Dad, you're such a knob.

MIKE: But you love me don't you?

BECKY: No.

MIKE: You don't wanna be looking for a bloke. You want to be concentrating on your singing. She's getting better all the time. Barry said...

BECKY: Listen to this Auntie Karen. You know that Glenda? She were practically shagging this skinny bloke in the pot plants.

KAREN: Oh yeah, Glenda don't mess about.

MIKE: Am I talking to meself here? I said Barry said you can do a solo any time you want.

BECKY: You ever been over Glenda's Dad? Four Irish wolfhounds in a council flat! Me and Lyn were there once, we had a seance, talked to the spirit of number five, the one Chub run over in his postie van.

MIKE: I reckon Chub had her.

BECKY: What? She shagged the bloke that ran over her dog?

MIKE: Yeah. I reckon he were a bit shaken, she were a bit upset, he came in for a cup of tea. No, I'm serious. I think Glenda succumbed to the masculine charms of my mate Chub.

BECKY: Give us a fag Dad.

MIKE: You've got to cut down on the fags an all if you wanna get anywhere with the singing…

BECKY: You joking? Fags are great for me voice. Make me all sexy.

She lights a fag and has a few drags. Sings the first few lines of Sheryl Crow's 'Strong Enough', exaggeratedly sexy.

CHARLIE runs in, holds out her Barbie Dictaphone and tapes BECKY as she sings.

MIKE: That's great love. Why won't you do that in the club?

BECKY continues singing.

CHARLIE: Sing more! Dad, sing with Becky, please!

MIKE: You call that dressed?

CHARLIE: Sing 'The way you hold your knife'!

MIKE and BECKY sing 'They Can't Take That Away From Me'. CHARLIE records them.

Sing 'Don't go breaking my heart'!

KAREN: Me and your Dad's got to get to the shop, it'll be getting busy.

MIKE: I'm serious about the singing love. You don't wanna be serving pizzas all your life do you?

BECKY: Yeah yeah.

KAREN and MIKE exit.

'You don't wanna be serving pizzas all your life, bla bla bla.'

CHARLIE: 'Bla bla beetroot, bla bla bla.'

BECKY: Dad's a twat int he?

CHARLIE: No, he's nice.

BECKY: You won't say that when you're my age.

CHARLIE: When I'm your age I'm gonna be a singer too. And I'm gonna be a vet.

BECKY: What, stick your hand up cows' arses? I'd rather serve pizzas.

CHARLIE: I think you should do a solo and be a famous singer. Cause you're as good as the people on the telly.

BECKY sings Sheryl Crow's 'All I Wanna Do.'

CHARLIE records it, then sings too.

They sing and dance, make up silly words, listen to themselves.

BECKY collapses, knackered.

CHARLIE lies down with her on the floor.

CHARLIE: Tell what Mum said about when it rains!

BECKY: Mum said when it rains it's the moon pissing.

CHARLIE: Tell about when the aliens are gonna come and adopt us as pets.

BECKY: Don't you ever get knackered Charlie?

CHARLIE: No. Tell about them aliens!

BECKY: Tomorrow.

Scene 5

Government office. ALAN and CAROLINE waiting to meet with the HEALTH MINISTER.

CAROLINE: Don't they even give you a cup of tea in here?

ALAN: A digestive biscuit would be nice.

HEALTH MINISTER enters, all shake hands.

HEALTH MINISTER: Sorry to keep you. No such thing as a simple answer to anything is there? Dr Harding. Nice to see you. How's Professor Harding? Ha ha.

CAROLINE: Fine thank you.

HEALTH MINISTER: I enjoyed that tennis tournament at the Mitchells'.

CAROLINE: Yes, it was lovely.

HEALTH MINISTER: So, I have your letters here. You do understand it was completely impossible for me to see you any sooner. My schedule…

ALAN: The trouble is, Minister, this is getting more urgent all the time. If you don't reinstate some of our funding you're going to be very unprepared if this turns out to be a serious health crisis.

HEALTH MINISTER: I'm going to be blunt with you Dr Andrews, and you understand that I'm not an expert. But how do we know it's going to?

CAROLINE: My unit's trying to evaluate the risk for you but since you reduced our staff all we can do is wait for doctors to refer cases to us.

ALAN: There's a paper that was published in Germany. It suggests that there might be an increase in cases of CJD in the UK in the next few years. And that this could be related to BSE.

CAROLINE: We think we might be seeing some patterns in the cases we're monitoring but we don't have enough to work with. If there's something going on you need to give us enough funding to find out what it is.

HEALTH MINISTER: If.

ALAN: It's quite possible that this could be an epidemic.

HEALTH MINISTER: I do understand that for you, this is very important. Because it's your careers and your livelihoods we're talking about. But for me, you see, it has to be weighed up alongside a lot of other health issues and some of them are killing a lot of people. It's not quite so simple if you look at the wider picture, is it? And that's what, in my position, I always have to do…

ALAN: I wasn't talking about my career!

CAROLINE: He was talking about an epidemic.

HEALTH MINISTER: Could you tell me how many other scientists in this country think there could be an epidemic?

CAROLINE: No scientist with any sense would close their mind to it.

HEALTH MINISTER: I don't see them all beating my door down Dr Harding.

ALAN: I'd say fifteen or twenty.

HEALTH MINISTER: All right. This is what I'm prepared to offer you. If you let me have the names of those fifteen or twenty then I will ensure that a proportion of them are invited to sit on our Spongiform Disease Investigation Committee. Which is a forum at which you will be able to raise these issues for debate at the highest level.

ALAN: Thank you.

CAROLINE: What about the funding?

HEALTH MINISTER: The recommendations of the SDIC are taken very seriously by the funding council. I hope that's satisfactory?

CAROLINE: I hope so too.

HEALTH MINISTER: Very glad to have been of service. Now I must rush, summoned for lunch with the Prime Minister again. Do give my regards to the Prof.

HEALTH MINISTER exits.

CAROLINE and ALAN laugh.

ALAN: Please tell me him and Tom aren't actually friends.

CAROLINE: He thinks they are. You think we'd have got to see him so quickly if he didn't?

ALAN: What are you doing with that man Caroline?

CAROLINE: Alan! Stop it.

Scene 6

Pub dressing room: KAREN doing BECKY's hair.

KAREN: Thing about Paul is he's fit but in a kind of boring way, you know? I mean I'm not saying I'd kick him out of bed.

BECKY: Except to shag him on the floor.

KAREN: Yeah. Whereas someone like… Promise you won't laugh.

BECKY is distracted.

Becky, you OK?

BECKY: Me head hurts.

KAREN: Have a paracetamol.

BECKY: Yeah.

KAREN: Look in my bag.

BECKY rummages in KAREN's bag.

Someone like Chub…

BECKY ignores her.

Have you not found them?

BECKY: What was I looking for?

She looks at KAREN, suddenly panicked. KAREN gives her a hug.

KAREN: It's all right pet, you're just nervous.

She feeds her a paracetamol and water.

BECKY: I should never have said I'd do this.

KAREN: You'll be fine.

Scene 7

Lights change. BECKY walks out into the pub, MIKE comes to meet her.

MIKE: I give you Rebecca Chapman!

MIKE sits in the audience/aisle.

BECKY goes to the mike.

BECKY: I'm going to do 'Missing.'

She sings four lines.

Pauses. Can't remember the words. Continues, next four lines.

Breaks off again.

Sorry. I… I…

She stumbles, has to grab hold of a chair.

Sorry.

She runs off, into the dressing room. Cries.

MIKE apologises to the audience, jumps up, goes to the dressing room.

MIKE: What's the problem love?

BECKY: Get out! What d'you think you're doing barging in on me?

MIKE: Just tell me what happened.

BECKY: (*Screaming in his face.*) I said get out!

Scene 8

The Inquiry. A shift happens: MIKE is propelled by BECKY's shout out of the dressing room and towards the inquiry, becomes the HEALTH MINISTER. BECKY becomes the CHAIR. We move forward three years to 1998 and the world changes to that of the inquiry.

CHAIR: Thank you Minister, that's all for the moment. Please be seated.

HEALTH MINISTER sits.

I wonder if Dr Harding will have any more success than you did, Minister, in casting her mind back three years to the time of this crisis? Dr Caroline Harding of the CJD Surveillance Unit.

CAROLINE comes up.

CHAIR: Dr Harding, you were a member of the Spongiform Disease Investigation Committee during 1995 and 96.

CAROLINE: Yes.

CHAIR: You have drawn our attention to a number of memos sent to the committee by the Health Minister during that time. Would you mind reading some of these?

CAROLINE: This one was after an article in the *Lancet* about CJD in farmers. The Chief Medical Officer then made a speech saying beef was safe and there was no link between BSE and CJD. It says: 'The Policy Unit has asked me to seek your advice as to whether there are likely to be any further cases of humans dying of apparently BSE-related illnesses and whether any firm medical evidence might emerge that disproves the link between BSE and CJD.'

CHAIR: Because at this stage there was no firm medical evidence of this sort?

CAROLINE: No. Not at any stage.

CHAIR: However the statements made by the Chief Medical Officer at the time were categorical in their assertions that there was no link between the two diseases.

CAROLINE: Yes.

CHAIR: Could you read us the November 1995 memo please?

CAROLINE: It says: 'The Prime Minister considers it essential that the government should be able to reassure consumers that British beef is safe to eat. I would therefore urge the committee to inform the government of research projects which might be able to confirm this view and to communicate to scientists working in the field that projects of this nature will be prioritised for government funding.'

CHAIR: And were you aware of any projects of this sort Dr Harding?

CAROLINE: We don't work to an agenda. That would be completely unethical.

CHAIR: Are you suggesting the government was trying to encourage scientists to behave in an unethical way?

CAROLINE: They tried to control what we said. If you didn't say what they wanted to hear you were the enemy. Like Alan. Dr Andrews. We all know what they did to him.

HEALTH MINISTER: I object! We did nothing whatsoever to Dr Andrews! All that is ridiculous speculation stirred up by the tabloid press!

Scene 9

MIKE's house. BECKY's room. BECKY sitting on her bed smoking. MIKE knocks on the door.

BECKY: What?

MIKE: That were Lyndsay on the phone again. Did you not ring her back? Can I come in love?

BECKY: Yeah.

MIKE comes in.

MIKE: You not going dancing tonight?

BECKY: No.

MIKE: Never known you to be in on a Saturday night. Ever since you were Charlie's age and we got you that bike. Remember? Didn't see you for days on end.

BECKY: BMX.

MIKE: Thought you were one of the lads dint you? Tell you what though, I never saw Jason Cousins or Gary Brown with as many scabby knees as you had.

BECKY: (*Halfhearted.*) You being sexist again Dad?

MIKE: What's up love? Look, I'm sorry if I made you do the singing when you weren't ready...

BECKY: Don't matter.

MIKE: You're not still upset about it?

BECKY: No.

MIKE: Why you not going out then, eh?

BECKY: I might go out. Might go to the garage for more fags.

MIKE: Smells like you've had plenty. Better open a window in here eh? Remember when you were about fourteen you used to think I didn't know you smoked. Standing by the window flapping a bit of paper going 'ooh I didn't like me new perfume.' Debbie wouldn't have liked that though, letting you smoke. Should've put me foot down.

BECKY: You wanted to scrounge me fags.

MIKE: Yeah. Listen love, if there's something up you can... I were young once too you know.

BECKY: (*Tired.*) I know Dad. You've still got a mental age of five.

MIKE: If it's something about a bloke you can tell me. I won't take the piss. Or talk to Karen if you can't talk to me. Don't like seeing you like this…

BECKY: Chill out Dad. Maybe I'm just getting a bit old for clubbing every weekend. Maybe I'm getting wise and responsible.

MIKE: I'm phoning the hospital!

BECKY: Or maybe it's PMT.

MIKE: Pissing Moon Trouble?

BECKY: That's the one.

Scene 10

Government office: ALAN and CAROLINE waiting for the HEALTH MINISTER.

ALAN: Come on then, let's see.

CAROLINE takes some photos of microscope slides out of a folder and shows him.

You were right.

CAROLINE: Every one of them the same, look. PrP plaques, but surrounded by spongiform change.

ALAN: Just like BSE. Tell him.

CAROLINE: Not till we've found more cases.

HEALTH MINISTER enters.

All shake hands.

HEALTH MINISTER: What can I do for my two most intelligent scientists today?

ALAN: It's about your speech.

HEALTH MINISTER: It went well I thought. No rotten eggs.

CAROLINE: (*Reads.*) 'In response to unsubstantiated scare stories in the press, the government would like to make it clear that there is absolutely no evidence that BSE causes CJD. There is no risk to human health from eating British beef or other meat products.'

HEALTH MINISTER: I thought it was clear, reassuring...

CAROLINE: There's been a terrible misunderstanding Minister. It was a very bad idea for you to say something like that.

HEALTH MINISTER: I was simply following the guidance of my scientific and policy advisors.

CAROLINE: We didn't say there's no risk.

HEALTH MINISTER: Correct me if I'm wrong here, but the impression I had was that nobody was able to provide any concrete evidence that there is a risk.

ALAN: Not yet, but we agreed it was possible!

HEALTH MINISTER: The advice I had from my civil servant was that the scientists were not able to agree at all on that point.

CAROLINE: We didn't get a hundred per cent consensus, but a lot of us think there probably is a risk.

ALAN: When you're dealing with risk that's enough. If you don't know then you shouldn't make a statement like the one you made.

HEALTH MINISTER: Do I take it that what you're suggesting I should do is go out there and say to the public that people have been catching this disease from British beef? When I have absolutely no scientific proof of that?

ALAN: What you should be saying is that you're not sure yet whether beef is safe so it's better to err on the side of caution.

HEALTH MINISTER: With respect, Dr Andrews, you don't understand politics.

Scene 11

MIKE's house. CHARLIE playing. BECKY in bed in her room. MIKE comes in with a beer and sits on the sofa, puts the telly on.

CHARLIE: Dad?

MIKE: Hmm?

CHARLIE: Why don't our Becky get up?

MIKE: Cause she's a lazy bugger.

CHARLIE: Dad, yesterday our Becky said she'd take me swimming but she never. Dad?

MIKE: What love?

CHARLIE: Our Becky don't like me no more.

MIKE: Course she likes you, you're her sister. Why don't you go in and see her, tell her you'll make her a cup of tea. Get your Dad some of them Monster Munches while you're at it.

CHARLIE goes into BECKY's room.

CHARLIE: Becky! Dad says you've got to get up and play with me.

BECKY: Play on your own.

CHARLIE: I'm bored playing on me own.

BECKY: D'you have to be so pathetic?

CHARLIE: Dad says you've got to get up cause it's nearly lunch time.

BECKY sighs, sits up.

BECKY: Pass me brush. Not that, that's a comb. The brush. All right then, I'm coming. Go on, go away.

CHARLIE: Becky?

BECKY: What?

CHARLIE: You said you'd do my hair in plaits.

BECKY: Not today, Charlie.

CHARLIE: But I've got Lisa's party tonight. I want my hair in plaits for Lisa's party! You said…

BECKY puts her head in her hands.

Becky, what's wrong?

BECKY: Nothing, sorry. What d'you want?

CHARLIE: My hair.

BECKY: Sit down there then.

BECKY looks at the brush as if frozen.

CHARLIE: Becky, will you tell the next bit of the aliens?

BECKY: Erm…where did we get to?

CHARLIE: It were his first day at the alien school.

BECKY: Yeah.

CHARLIE: My hair!

BECKY: OK.

BECKY starts brushing CHARLEY's hair.

CHARLIE: He were worried about going to the alien school cause he couldn't get a uniform to fit him cause of not having eight legs.

BECKY: Yes, he didn't have eight legs, so he went to the ghost master and said…

CHARLIE: The ghost master int in it!

BECKY is absently tangling the brush in CHARLEY's hair.

The ghost master's in the afterlife story, Becky, this is the alien invasion story.

BECKY tries to pull the brush down but it's tangled up.

CHARLIE: Ow! You're hurting!

BECKY: Sorry. Look, I just have to lie down. Go and play with your dolls.

She lies down.

CHARLIE comes away, goes into the living room, plays with her Barbie dolls, makes them speak.

CHARLIE:

Barbie 2: 'All I wanna do is have some fun.'
Where's my pink scrunchie and body glitter?

Barbie 1: I didn't get it.

Barbie 2: You 'ant brought owt, not even sweets.

Barbie 2: Shut up and go away. I int going in town shopping ever again, I'm just staying at home.

BECKY comes downstairs.

BECKY: Can you turn that TV down?

MIKE: You joking? You can't hear it up there.

BECKY: It's loud. I can hear it.

MIKE: I can hardly hear it meself.

CHARLIE: Becky, come and play Barbies.

BECKY: No.

CHARLIE: (*As Barbie 1.*) She's a right mardy moo. (*Singing, as dolls.*) I'm a mardy cow and I go moo, moo moo moo, moo.

BECKY: Shut up! Dad, tell her to shut up.

MIKE: Quiet Charlie, you're upsetting your sister. She's developed superhuman hearing.

CHARLIE: (*Whispering.*) Moo moo moo.

BECKY: If you don't shut up.

CHARLIE: Dad, Becky's being funny again. (*To BECKY.*) I don't like you no more. Dad, she's funny.

BECKY: Will you just fucking shut up!

CHARLIE covers her mouth with her hand, shocked.

CHARLIE: Dad, Becky swore at me.

BECKY: 'Dad, Becky swore at me.' Little brat.

MIKE: Since when did you think swearing at kids was clever?

BECKY: She keeps making stupid noises.

MIKE: She's only nine.

BECKY: So? She can stand up for herself.

CHARLIE: No I can't.

MIKE: You can't be like this round her.

BECKY: I'm not being like owt, she's just playing up.

MIKE: No, you're playing up. Sitting in your room all day with the curtains shut. What am I supposed to do, if you won't tell me what's up? You've got your mates ringing up every day. I don't know what to say to them.

BECKY: Say what you like. Say I've run away with the circus.

CHARLIE: Dad, Becky swore yesterday an' all. She said the word you're only meant to say after nine o' clock but she said it at lunch time.

MIKE: What's all this about, eh?

BECKY: Nowt.

MIKE: Charlie, your big sister's really sorry she shouted at you. Int you Becky?

BECKY: Yeah.

MIKE: Go on then.

BECKY: Sorry I shouted Charlie.

MIKE: Come here, why don't we all have a hug? We have to agree that we're going to be nice to Becky.

CHARLIE: Why?

MIKE: Just because.

CHARLIE: But…

MIKE: Shhh.

CHARLIE: Dad, is Becky coming to the fair tomorrow?

MIKE: Are you coming?

BECKY shakes her head.

She don't know. No more World War Threes all right?

CHARLIE: D'you wanna play?

BECKY shakes her head.

MIKE: Leave your sister alone for a bit, Charlie. Read your puzzle book or summat.

BECKY sits on the sofa with MIKE.

He turns the TV down low.

CHARLIE: 'All I wanna do is have some fun
I got a feeling…'

BECKY jumps up and hits CHARLIE round the head.

MIKE: Rebecca!

CHARLIE wails.

MIKE hugs her.

BECKY: She never shuts up! No one ever shuts up round here. It does my fucking head in!

MIKE: If you touch her one more time you can go. You can pack your bags and go to your Auntie Karen's.

BECKY: Fine. I don't care. I don't give a fuck.

MIKE: If you swear at me once more I'll pack them for you.

BECKY: Fuck, fuck, fuck, fuck, fuck.

MIKE: OK.

BECKY: I don't want to fucking stay here anyway.

She exits.

CHARLIE: Why's our Becky funny dad?

MIKE: I don't know.

Scene 12

KAREN's house. BECKY sitting on the sofa, staring into space. Switches the TV on then seems to forget about it, keeps staring into space. Snaps out of it and changes channels. Gets distracted again. Suddenly starts to cry. Curls up into a ball. KAREN comes in, faffs around a bit before noticing BECKY.

KAREN: Oh you're there love. Want a cuppa? You sleeping? Becky?

She sits down next to her.

BECKY pulls away from her.

Hey, what is it? You can talk to me. Your Dad's right. It's like you've had a personality transplant. Where's our Becky, eh?

Puts her hand on BECKY. BECKY shakes it away.

BECKY suddenly jumps up from the sofa and jumps up and down.

BECKY: Ow! Shit!

KAREN: What is wrong with you?

BECKY: I've got pins and needles. Really bad. Ow.

KAREN: I'm not surprised if you've been sitting there all day.

BECKY: You don't understand. None of you understand! I'm… There's… It's not right, I'm not light, there's something long.

KAREN bursts out laughing.

Don't laugh! I'm serious. What did I say?

KAREN: You're on something int you? What have you bleeding taken? I never thought you did drugs Becks. Your poor Dad…

BECKY: I 'ant taken drugs! I've got cancer!

She bursts into tears.

48

KAREN: You 'ant got cancer love.

BECKY: How do you know?

KAREN: Are you in pain?

BECKY: My legs feel funny.

KAREN: You're not pregnant are you?

BECKY: I won't never have kids. Cause I'm going to die of cancer.

KAREN: I'm going to the Co-op to get one of them tests.

BECKY: Do they sell a test for cancer in the Co-op?

KAREN: No! A pregnancy test!

BECKY: Don't be daft Auntie Karen. You know 'ant had a shag since Lyndsay's birthday.

KAREN: Right.

BECKY: I woke up last night and there were a feeling in my leg. Like it were…

Pause.

KAREN: Like it were what?

BECKY shrugs, has forgotten what she was saying.

KAREN strokes her arm.

Scene 13

The Inquiry.

CHAIR: You tried to persuade Chancellor Kohl to back down over restrictions on imports of British beef and what was his response?

HEALTH MINISTER: That he was under political pressure not to.

CHAIR: And how did you interpret that response?

HEALTH MINISTER: It was complete nonsense. That ban was illegal. It undermined the principles of the single market.

CHAIR: It wasn't because his scientific advisors had told him British beef wasn't safe?

HEALTH MINISTER: This is not as simple as you're implying. There are economic considerations. The Germans are our competitors. They had a vested interest in saying it wasn't safe.

CHAIR: Perhaps you could read us the memo you sent to the Prime Minister on the subject?

HEALTH MINISTER: 'Chancellor Kohl's response is that in the opinion of German experts, BSE could also pose a risk to humans, although the extent of this risk and the conclusions to be drawn are a matter of contention.'

CHAIR: So the Germans told you they thought there could be a risk. Remind us of the date Minister.

HEALTH MINISTER: June 16th 1994.

CHAIR: And you finally did announce that risk to the British public in June 1996. Please read the next part of the memo.

HEALTH MINISTER: 'The Agriculture Minister and myself are concerned that any new restrictions introduced by us at this time, whether or not scientifically based, would be interpreted as Britain bowing to German political pressure.'

CHAIR: So new restrictions were not introduced?

HEALTH MINISTER: No.

Scene 14

KAREN's house: KAREN and MIKE.

MIKE: We're mates, me and Becks. We don't fight.

KAREN: It's maybe…her age or summat.

MIKE: D'you reckon I were too hard on her, chucking her out? She were out of order though. I can't let her swear at Charlie can I?

KAREN: No.

MIKE: D'you reckon I spoil her?

KAREN: No, I reckon…

MIKE: Maybe I've made it all too cosy and now she's got herself in a state cause she might have to get a real job and do the singing and that.

KAREN: Maybe you push her too much, Mike, with the singing.

MIKE: Yeah, but she's good!

KAREN: I know, but she int like you. She int ambitious like that.

MIKE: A dad's got to be ambitious for his kids though, 'ant he? They can do so much stuff we could never do. But they don't do it. They just sit on their arses.

KAREN: She kept saying she had pains. I said are you pregnant?

MIKE: She 'ant had a shag since what's her name's birthday!

KAREN: I asked her if she were on drugs.

MIKE: She int on drugs!

KAREN: I think it might be summat to do with her mam.

MIKE: It's been five years. Why now?

KAREN: I dunno.

MIKE: What've I done wrong, eh?

KAREN: Nothing Mike. I think she's maybe depressed. I'm taking her to the doctor. I think you should come an all. I got a cancellation for tomorrow.

MIKE: The doctor? What the bloody hell for?

KAREN: Maybe she needs some help.

MIKE: What, you mean see a shrink?

KAREN: A psychiatrist Mike. You watch too much American telly.

MIKE: Nah, it must be summat else.

KAREN: There's another thing. Sometimes she's been mixing her words up.

BECKY has come downstairs, dopey. Stands in the doorway.

MIKE: Come in here love.

KAREN: Come and sit down.

BECKY starts to walk into the room. Her leg buckles under her and she falls.

MIKE picks BECKY up and carries her to bed in the hospital.

Scene 15

Leeds hospital: BECKY in bed, tired. CHARLIE wandering about.

CHARLIE: When's Dad and Auntie Karen coming back?

BECKY: I told you I don't know. They've got to talk to the doctor.

CHARLIE: I'm bored.

BECKY: That makes two of us then. Sit down Charlie.

CHARLIE: I hate hospital. Everyone's always telling me to sit down.

BECKY: I hate hospital cause they stick needles in me.

CHARLIE: Why?

BECKY: To see what's wrong with me.

CHARLIE: Are you on drugs? Dad said there was nowt wrong with you, he said you were just mardy cause of your age and cause you work in Pizza Hut and then Auntie Karen said maybe you're on drugs. I heard them.

BECKY: I'm not on drugs.

CHARLIE: Lisa says you've got cancer like Mam.

BECKY: That's nice.

CHARLIE: Lisa says you have to be really poorly to fall over for no reason like what you did. Dad got lots of stuff off the Internet and he says it's OK if you've got cancer cause you still might not die.

BECKY: Cheers.

CHARLIE: I had to show Dad how to do it, he didn't know owt. He couldn't do the double click, he were going like this. That maths test the doctor made you do were easier than the ones we do at school. When you've got cancer does that mean you can't do maths no more? Or Dad said the doctor said you might have MS and he looked that up an all and he said they can make it better cause they can give you a tablet that makes it better or summat, but it might take a long time, like two months or two years. Becky?

BECKY: Stop asking questions Charlie.

CHARLIE: Why d'you have to wear that paper dress? I can see your pants at the back.

Scene 16

Inquiry/Leeds hospital: MIKE and KAREN sit in the doctor's office. They respond to an imaginary doctor giving them the diagnosis. CAROLINE speaks to the inquiry.

MIKE: They always keep you waiting don't they?

CAROLINE: What I and the other researchers identified and presented in that paper in the *Lancet* in 1996 was that there was a new variant of Creuzfeld Jakob Disease, which had a different clinical course as well as different neuropathology. Patients are all relatively young when symptoms first appear, an average age of 29, and the duration from diagnosis until death is longer, a year on average.

MIKE: It's cancer int it?

CAROLINE: These cases were so distinct and the disease is so rare that initially many of them weren't diagnosed as CJD by doctors. It was only later that some were referred to the CJD Surveillance Unit, sometimes only after death.

MIKE: So it's like a brain tumour then?

KAREN: I think it's meat int it, it's mad cow disease and eating beef. It's everywhere on the Internet.

CAROLINE: None of the cases had a history of potential exposure to CJD through neurosurgery or human pituitary-derived hormones and none had had a blood transfusion. One had been a strict vegetarian since 1991 but all had eaten beef or beef products within the last ten years.

MIKE: Is there a cure?

There int is there?

CAROLINE: We stressed that we were not presenting direct evidence of a link between BSE and this new variant of CJD. However we concluded that: 'exposure to the BSE agent is perhaps the most plausible interpretation of our findings'.

MIKE: It don't matter what it costs. I'll pay for it.

BECKY walks across the stage. She stumbles.

CHARLIE appears, rushes to help her.

They walk slowly, CHARLIE supporting BECKY. Towards the end BECKY ushers CHARLIE away.

CHARLIE goes and sits.

BECKY walks on her own to sit next to CHARLIE. She is slow and wobbly. BECKY curls up on the sofa.

CHARLIE puts a blanket over her.

Music: BECKY singing 'Strong Enough'.

End of Act One.

ACT TWO

Scene 1

MIKE's comedy routine. MIKE talks as if he's in the pub but behind him the New York Hospital is being created. BECKY in bed, nurses and doctors running around, shouting to each other, sometimes coming in front of him with equipment etc.

MIKE: (*Eating a meat pie.*) Sorry I'm late, had to grab a pie on the way here. Haven't been getting me dinner cooked for me lately. The missus is still training the ferret.

Don't tell me daughter I'm eating this, all right? I was having one the other night and she's there going don't eat that Dad, you'll get that nvCJD. Hands up who here knows what nvCJD is. Hands up who don't know. Hands up who don't give a fuck. It's mad cow disease int it? Yeah, the mother-in-law's had it as long as I've known her and they reckon she's passed it onto cows now. Mad cow disease, Bovine Spongiform Encephalopathy. I mean who thinks these fucking names up? I prefer mad cow, at least you can still say it when you're pissed.

Me daughter says you can get it from mechanically recovered meat products. I asked if that meant the RAC scraping up roadkill and selling it on. She says no you can get it from a meat pie but they're not sure how. So I'm thinking is it like AIDS, you know, you have to get the pie in your blood stream, you have to cut yourself on the pie, or you have to inject the pie? Is there pie junkies out there, sharing a pie? Or d'you have to have sex with the pie without using a condom? Unprotected pie sex. I don't know. It'll be illegal soon, they'll be arresting you for eating a meat pie, there'll be people on street corners offering you a pie. There'll be the dealers down Gipton going 'Es, whiz, pies', pie dealers driving around at night shooting it out for control of the pie territory. 'Don't fuck with my pie.'

There's no rhyme or reason is there? I've eaten so many dodgy pies in me time you'd think I'd be a dead cert but I'm all right int I? Don't answer that Madam. I told them I must've eaten a lorryload of cow spine, I told them I'd once cut meself very badly on a tin of corned beef, I told them that once, on a particularly inebriated stag do in Skegness, I'd shagged a lukewarm pasty in the absence of female companionship. But they just shrugged their shoulders. It's daft int it? It's proper fucking food, a meat pie. Proper old fashioned food.

She's a laugh is our Becky.

She uh…she int singing tonight.

Scene 2

The Inquiry.

CHAIR: Minister, it was the job of one of your civil servants to sit on the Spongiform Disease Investigation Committee and summarise the scientists' discussions for ministers.

HEALTH MINISTER: Yes.

CHAIR: We have copies of e-mails sent by yourself to that civil servant during 1995 and 96. Could you please read the first highlighted section to us?

HEALTH MINISTER: This is simply me giving her the background about the scientists…

CHAIR: I would like you to read the highlighted section to us please.

HEALTH MINISTER: This is all out of context! 'Dr Pritchard has been with us since the beginning of the

57

BSE crisis and always makes cautious and measured statements. He comes from a farming family and is the owner of a chain of slaughterhouses and therefore understands the government's commitment to the interests of farming and business. His are the best opinions to be passed on to the Policy Unit. Please keep me abreast privately of any alarmist statements made by other members, principally Dr Wright and Dr Harding, who seem to believe that we are looking at some sort of health crisis. It is best not to minute these sort of statements at this stage.'

CHAIR: Why were you seeking to censor information, Minister?

HEALTH MINISTER: I was not censoring information. I was operating within a political system and that is how a political system works. Everything the government does fits into a policy framework. I get guidance from above about government policy and I have to act accordingly.

CHAIR: And your guidance from above was telling you, in this case…?

HEALTH MINISTER: That we wanted to avoid serious damage to the beef industry.

CHAIR: Thank you. Could I call Katie Conway, reporter at the *Daily Post* newspaper?

KATIE goes up.

Miss Conway, you were one of a number of journalists who put pressure on the government to address this issue through your coverage of possible cases. I believe your involvement was with one particular family?

KATIE: Yes. I had a really strong feeling about the story right from the start. Maybe cause my granny's from Bradford and I understand the way of life in the North, you know? The father, Mike, he's a really inspirational guy. When he got the diagnosis he didn't give up, he went straight on the net and tried to find out who could treat this disease. And he found Professor Jack Liebermann working with a drug called quinacrine in the US. He gave me a call and I went to see him and he said 'Katie, I talked to Jack Liebermann and he's invited us to the US.' Just like that. So that's how the *Post* got involved and I managed to persuade my editor to fund the trip for Becky and Mike. Because this was a story about amazing human determination in the face of tragedy, which is just amazing for our readers.

Scene 3

New York press conference. JACK, MIKE and BECKY on a stage. BECKY in a wheelchair, visibly sicker.

JACK: Our studies show that tricyclic compounds with an aliphatic side chain at the middle ring moiety constitute a new class of anti-prion reagents. Because quinacrine has been used in humans for many years as an anti-malarial drug, and is known to pass the blood-brain barrier, we suggest that it is an immediate candidate for the treatment of Creutzfeldt Jakob disease.

Clapping.

Questions?

SCIENTIFIC EXPERT: Professor Liebermann, will the brain, even if successfully cleared of these rogue prions, be able to stage a repair-job on the damaged nerve cells?

JACK: That is something we don't fully understand at present. But the improvement in brain and motor function we have observed in this patient is unprecedented. I think we may proceed with cautious optimism.

KATIE: Will New York's state of the art Institute for Brain Disease hold the cure for one brave British teenager's horrific and unexplained disease?

Beautiful Becky Chapman is seventeen, a talented performer who was about to embark on a glittering career in London's West End. But now Becky has fallen prey to a mysterious and cruel disease. It's called Creuzfeld Jakob Disease and it normally only strikes in old age.

JACK: When she arrived here Rebecca had very little motor function.

MIKE: We hadn't seen her walk for weeks. It were heart-breaking. It all happened so fast.

KATIE: In just three months, Becky had deteriorated from a lively, perky young woman to a bed-ridden invalid requiring constant care. But her father Mike took a last desperate gamble and took Becky to Nobel Prize-winning Professor Jack Liebermann. The *Post* was with him all the way.

MIKE: Professor Liebermann believes there's hope, you know, and that's what no one in Britain were prepared to do, they all wanted us to give up. Didn't they love? She 'ant walked for three weeks and she walked yesterday for him. He came in, I helped her up, and he just goes, 'Hello Becky. Can you walk over here and see me?' And she did.

KATIE: Can Becky talk to us now?

MIKE: Course she can. Say hello to the journalists love.

BECKY: Hello to the journalists love.

MIKE: She's always taking the piss.

KATIE: How are you feeling Becky?

MIKE: She's a bit tired after all the tests this morning.

KATIE: Have you been feeling better since you came to America?

MIKE: Let's show them the thing with the hands, shall we?

JACK: This is a co-ordination test I have been asking Rebecca to do for me which she found impossible when she first arrived.

MIKE: Come on Becky, the thing with the hands. That's it.

BECKY copies MIKE in the hand test where you turn one hand face up then face down repeatedly on the other palm.

Do it quicker love. Like you were doing this morning.

KATIE: Oh, that's lovely.

MIKE: She can do it much quicker than that, she were doing it twice as quick this morning.

KATIE: She's a real fighter isn't she?

MIKE: Yeah, she int gonna give up. Nor's her Dad.

KATIE: The two of you are such an incredible example…

SCIENTIFIC EXPERT: So if the damage can't be repaired then the most the patient's going to get is a slowing or halting of the progress of the disease?

JACK: Yes.

MIKE: Then we do this one where you touch the nose. Come on Becky, concentrate for me. Touch your nose.

KATIE: Oh she's tired, bless her. Should we let her rest now?

MIKE: No, she's fine, she's got to practise it. The more we practise it the quicker she gets better. That's right, int it doctor? Come on, touch your nose.

He demonstrates. BECKY doesn't respond.

SCIENTIFIC EXPERT: Is it correct that a second patient given the drugs showed no sign of improvement whatsoever?

JACK: That is correct, yes.

MIKE: I always liked to think a miracle could happen, and now it has.

KATIE: Mike told the *Post* exclusively today.

JACK: This is totally new for us and really quite remarkable.

KATIE: Professor Liebermann told the *Post*.

BECKY reaches out and touches MIKE's nose.

Laughter from the audience.

Scene 4

ALAN's lab: KAREN in ALAN's lab, ALAN searching through papers.

ALAN: This one's Liebermann's own paper. But it's very scientific.

KAREN: Just give me everything you've got about it. Please.

ALAN: The experiments described here were done in test tubes. I don't know how relevant this… I'm not sure where page five is.

KAREN: This is really kind of you Dr Andrews.

ALAN: I think… I'm so sorry, I think you're sat on page five.

KAREN stands up.

Oh, here's another one. This might be of interest too.

KAREN: I think you need a secretary.

ALAN: Yes, you're right. That's one of the things I need but the government's not too keen on giving me enough funding at the moment.

KAREN: That's terrible.

ALAN: Well it's worrying because there's a need for the treatments I'm working on, there might be an increasing need…

KAREN: How do you mean?

ALAN: Oh I'm sorry. I get carried away about this. I haven't even offered you a cup of tea.

KAREN: That's OK. I don't want to be any trouble.

ALAN: It's no trouble. I could do with some myself. The problem is I don't have access to the information you need either. Dr Liebermann keeps his work quite close to his chest.

KAREN: Shall I make the tea?

ALAN: Oh, thank you, yes.

KAREN makes tea.

KAREN: I don't want to take up too much of your time.

ALAN: On the contrary, I'm very glad you found me. I'd like to do anything I can…and you could help a friend of mine too, at the CJD Surveillance Unit, if you wouldn't mind answering some questions for her research.

KAREN: OK.

ALAN: She'd really need Becky's notes too but I suppose that'll have to wait. How's the treatment going?

KAREN: Mike says she's walked. Which is amazing. Before she went away she were really wobbly. We had to lift her all the time. And her talking had got funny an' all, and dribbling…it's horrible int it?

ALAN: I think it's a very good thing your niece is having this treatment Karen. I just wish it were over here and I could be there.

KAREN: Me too.

She hands him his tea.

Scene 5

New York hospital: MIKE, BECKY, KATIE. BECKY concentrates hard to follow the conversation. KATIE laughs at all of MIKE's jokes.

MIKE: I reckon the only thing that's bigger than religion in this place is food. Int it love? They're either on some mad diet where you can only eat macrobiotic kumquats on a Friday if it's a full moon or they're knocking back super massive family-sized McDonald's with triple fries and a bucket of lard milkshake.

BECKY: Kumquats in a full moon.

MIKE: Yeah, that's right. Kumquats in a full moon. When I'm in the street here I'm the only normal person around.

BECKY: You int normal Dad.

KATIE: Aw, you're right Becky, he's not is he? He's a really special Dad.

BECKY: Special…needs.

MIKE: Oi! I tell you though, everyone else either looks like a twiglet or a bouncy castle. Hey, you're looking a bit skinny an all, int she Katie?

KATIE: Maybe a bit.

MIKE: Got to keep trying to eat love. D'you not like the food here?

BECKY: Yeah, I like it. I like the...

MIKE: The what? Them great big sandwiches?

BECKY: No the...

MIKE: The ones that have to have a cocktail stick to hold it all together?

BECKY: No, the...

KATIE: Those pancake things.

BECKY: The kumquats.

MIKE: You daft bugger.

BECKY: I forget all the words Dad.

MIKE: Give the doctor a few weeks love and you'll be remembering everything.

JACK enters.

JACK: Morning Mike. Everything all right here?

MIKE: Fantastic doctor. OK if Katie stays?

JACK: If that's all right with you and Becky.

MIKE: Yeah, yeah. Katie's gonna tell everyone at home how well you're doing love. Ready to walk again? End of the corridor, remember?

JACK: How are you feeling Becky?

BECKY: Sick.

MIKE: She just has to get used to it don't she? Her body just has to get used to the drugs.

JACK: That's right. Do you feel you can try a little walking Becky?

BECKY: I don't know.

MIKE: Come on love.

BECKY moves to the edge of the bed and stands up holding MIKE's arm.

That's my girl.

JACK: Like we did yesterday Becky. See if you can take a walk over here. Your Dad's right there behind you.

MIKE lets go.

BECKY stands. Concentrates.

KATIE is completely gripped.

KATIE: Come on sweetheart.

BECKY reaches out for MIKE again.

BECKY: I can't.

MIKE: You can love! She always thinks she can't do it. She's never gonna get better if she thinks she can't do it is she?

BECKY: I'm tired.

JACK: How about a few steps with Dad holding your arm then Becky?

MIKE takes BECKY's arm again.

She takes one wobbly step.

That's just great.

KATIE: Brilliant.

She takes two more wobbly steps.

MIKE: Fantastic! See?

JACK: Now on your own Becky. Come on over to me.

BECKY stands. Shakes her head.

MIKE: Come on Becks. Tell you what, you do a step, I'll give you a fag for later.

BECKY does a step.

JACK: Good.

MIKE: Carry on love. OK, OK, another fag. Fag for every step, all right?

BECKY walks seven more steps, getting more uncoordinated the more she walks, to JACK.

KATIE claps. She has got quite tearful.

KATIE: Oh that's wonderful!

JACK: Five steps. That's real good.

MIKE: Brilliant love.

They get her back to bed.

All that time I couldn't get her to do one step and now she's doing five! Once she's started she don't stop, does she? Let's hope she don't end up doing a marathon. Cost me a fortune in fags.

KATIE: It's amazing.

KATIE wipes away tears.

MIKE hugs her.

MIKE: You're going to see lots more where that came from Katie.

JACK: I'm real pleased with Becky's progress, Mike. We're gonna keep monitoring her very closely. You're aware of the possible risks...

MIKE: We're willing to take them. I just want to see the old Becky again.

JACK: You know we can't guarantee anything, Mike, but you're at the top hospital in the world for this.

MIKE: I told her that, I told her she's in the best place.

Scene 6

KAREN, ALAN and CHARLIE picking daisies and putting them in a bin bag.

KAREN: Mike's always got a funny story. He told me last night Becky pressed the emergency buzzer on her bed and all the nurses came running and she said she wanted to order a pizza. I don't even know if that's true.

CHARLIE: Bet it were four seasons. Can we have pizza tonight?

KAREN: Maybe if you pick lots and lots of daisies.

CHARLIE: Why can't Dr Alan make Becky better here?

ALAN: I haven't worked out how yet.

CHARLIE: Why can't the man in America tell you?

KAREN: Because he wants to keep it all to himself so he can get famous.

CHARLIE: Will Becky be famous?

KAREN: We just want her better love.

CHARLIE: I'm going to make her better with a ginormous daisy chain.

KAREN: What can you do with daisies?

ALAN: There's something I can extract from the leaves, called alkaloidal glycosidase inhibitors. They're very expensive, they normally get them from exotic plants. And obviously I've got no money for chemicals now they're not funding me.

KAREN: You found these things in daisies?

ALAN: I tried a few plants. I knew it'd be somewhere.

KAREN: You're right clever.

ALAN: I don't know. I think I might have been very naïve. You know I gave them a list of the scientists who are concerned about there being a connection between BSE and CJD. And do you know how many of them had their funding applications rejected?

KAREN: How many?

ALAN: All of them. Caroline's unit, the Surveillance Unit, they're still being funded but it's a massive cut. It's going to really slow their work down. And I wrote to all those scientists on the list, asking them to send a letter to the press with me, expressing concern. None of them would. They were worried about their careers.

KAREN: We have to do summat.

ALAN: You are. You're helping me pick daisies. We're not going to let them stop us. Are we Charlie?

CHARLIE: How many daisies to make Becky better?

ALAN: I'm afraid I just can't say.

Scene 7

NY hospital: MIKE talking to BECKY

MIKE: Went into this sex shop yesterday. God it scared the shit out of me. Nah, I know what you're thinking, I just wandered in out of curiosity, thought I might get your Auntie Karen something for a laugh. But this woman wouldn't leave me alone. Kept going, 'Are you looking for videos Sir? What kind of videos do you prefer?' And they've got like farmyard stuff and all sorts, I was that embarrassed. And there's me trying to get to the door and she's following me, going, 'Is it for yourself Sir?' So I go no it's for me sister-in-law and she gets out this huge black dildo.

BECKY whimpers, holds her head.

What's up love?

BECKY: My head, it's like…

She looks for the words but gives up.

MIKE: That cause I'm talking rubbish eh?

BECKY laughs weakly.

BECKY: Yeah.

MIKE: What sort of pain is it? Then we can tell the doctor. Is it like a stabbing pain?

BECKY: I don't know.

BECKY starts to cry.

MIKE: Hey, hey, it's all right. Have a drink of water. You've got to drink lots of water.

BECKY: No.

MIKE: Come on. It's good for you love.

BECKY: I can't think! I'm dying! I'm going to die Dad!

MIKE: Shhh. No you're not. You're going to fight it. You hear me? We're going to fight it together.

BECKY: I can't!

MIKE: You can. I know you can.

BECKY: You don't know. You're wrong Dad. I'm not…

MIKE: Hey, hey.

BECKY: (*Words all mixed up.*) You're not fighting me Dad!

MIKE: Shh. There's the doc. I'll go and see if he can do anything. OK?

MIKE intercepts JACK.

Have you got a sec, doc? It's just that she int too happy today. The pills 'ant worked for her head, it's still killing her. And the other thing is she was going on this morning about how she still can't pee, I think that's what she was saying.

JACK: That's an effect of the amytriptaline. On balance, though, there are distinct advantages to that drug as an anti-depressant in this case…

MIKE: You're right, she's yellow, int she? I can see it now. Is that like jaundice? She had that when she were a baby.

JACK: No, that's just colouration from the drug. The drug spreads through the body like a dye.

MIKE: Will it go away?

JACK: Not for some time, but it won't harm her. I examined her eyes earlier as we need to check for any yellow pigmentation there.

MIKE: She's too sick to have a fag. She's taking that pretty bad.

JACK: I know some of this is distressing, Mike but we're not dealing with anything that suggests a serious toxic reaction. I can increase the painkillers a little for the headache. Now take a break, Mike, get yourself something to eat.

MIKE: I'm not hungry, thanks.

JACK: I think it would be good idea to let Becky rest a little now. Tomorrow we've got an EKG and a lumber puncture lined up as well as the MRI, so we need her to be fresh.

MIKE: I'll just sit with her doc. I won't disturb her, honest.

JACK: I think the best thing would be if you were to go back to your hotel and try to relax, Mike. Take a bath, order in, watch some TV.

MIKE: I keep telling you doctor, I'm not tired.

JACK: You may not feel tired Mike but you've had very little sleep in the last forty-eight hours. What we always say to relatives is quality time, not all the time. You're most useful to her when you're at your best.

MIKE: Yeah, all right. I might just give Karen a ring then.

JACK exits.

MIKE goes to BECKY.

She is curled up in a ball and seems to be sleeping.

The doctor's going to come and give you something else for your head love. OK? I might just pop off for a bit. Hope that's OK.

He kisses BECKY, exits.

Scene 8

KAREN, ALAN, CHARLIE with their bin bag in a field.

CHARLIE: Alan, tell about how plants breathe.

ALAN: No. I don't believe it.

KAREN: Where have they gone?

CHARLIE: Maybe cows have eaten them. Not mad cows, just normal cows. Cause mad cows don't eat daisies, they eat chocolate muffins and ice cream.

KAREN: Shhh Charlie.

CHARLIE: But they should eat daisies cause it'd make them better. Stupid cows.

ALAN: This is a nightmare.

CHARLIE: Or someone else is collecting them too.

ALAN: Exactly. Whichever of their cronies they've decided to fund instead of me. They're trying to stop me.

ALAN sits down on the ground.

CHARLIE: How will we get the daisies inside our Becky's head?

KAREN: You go over by the trees and pick some dandelions love. You know which ones they are?

CHARLIE: (*To ALAN.*) Do dandelions work an' all?

ALAN: We can give it a go.

CHARLIE exits.

KAREN sits down.

KAREN: There can't have been any daisies here. You must've got confused.

ALAN: There were. They've taken them.

KAREN: Who?

ALAN: The government.

KAREN: Why would they do that?

ALAN: Because I've said things they don't like. It's not just the daisies. I was at the lab yesterday and they'd run out of potassium hydroxide. That's never happened before. And then my account had mysteriously disappeared from their computer and they told me I need to update my authorisation from the funding council. Which of course I can't.

KAREN: Really?

ALAN: They're spying on me too. I did a talk to Chemistry students at the university last week. At the back of the room there was this woman making notes. I've seen her before when Caroline and I went to see the Health Minister. She's one of his civil servants. I ran after her at the end but she drove off about seventy miles an hour.

KAREN: You need to tell someone. Tell the press.

ALAN: I've got no evidence. I don't know about this sort of thing Karen. I know about antioxidants and COX-2 inhibition. And now they've taken my glycosidase inhibitors away.

KAREN: What can I do Alan? I've written to my MP. The petition's going well, there's people e-mailing all the time. Really horrible stories. There was a boy who died of CJD a couple of months ago. He were fifteen. The hospital wouldn't have him so he died in an old folks' home.

ALAN: You must put them all in touch with Caroline.

KAREN: I will. I could write to the Health Minister too. Tell me what to say.

CHARLIE runs up.

Are you all right love?

CHARLIE: I just got a bit sad again.

KAREN: About your sister?

CHARLIE: No. I was thinking about them mice again.

ALAN: I tell you what Charlie, you're right. It's not very nice to the mice.

CHARLIE: He tries out diseases on them Auntie Karen.

KAREN: I know.

CHARLIE: I don't like it.

ALAN: We'll go back to the lab now and get them. The well ones that is. And we'll bring them here and let them out.

CHARLIE: Yes!

She hugs him.

What about the ill ones?

ALAN: Well, I'll keep trying to make them better and if I can't we'll just have to look after them until they die.

ALAN hugs CHARLIE.

KAREN takes CHARLEY's hand.

Scene 9

NY hospital: JACK's office. MIKE waiting. JACK enters.

JACK: Morning Mike. Sleeping OK?

MIKE: Oh, yeah, brilliant doctor, eight hours a night, no problem.

JACK: Becky's looking good. We have the nausea under control, she ate breakfast this morning and yesterday. No worsening in the left eye. And she has another session with the speech therapist this afternoon to look at the gurgling. Now I have her MRI scans here. You'll remember we did a scan of the brain when you arrived here three weeks ago. That's this one.

JACK displays brain scan.

The dark area here is where the disease has caused the death of nerve cells. Now if we compare this with yesterday's scan, which is this one...

JACK displays second scan.

MIKE: Oh my God. That's incredible doctor, that's amazing!

JACK: As you can see there is a reduction in the dark area of about one fifth.

KATIE comes on.

KATIE: The brain is recovering! It's re-growing!

MIKE: You're brilliant! Thank you so much! Becky'll be so chuffed, she'll be over the moon.

KATIE: The brain tissue is literally re-forming itself!

JACK: We're very excited about this too Mike, but you do understand we're in completely new territory here. We just don't know how this treatment's going to develop. This is a bit like Captain Kirk from the Enterprise making his first light speed jump.

MIKE: Well, you just go right ahead and jump, doctor, go and get them prion baddies, we've got complete faith in you. Boldly go where no man has gone before!

JACK: Yes. No *one*. That's what they say now isn't it?

JACK exits, goes to BECKY's bed, consults charts.

KATIE: It looks like positive results all the way!

MIKE and KATIE hug.

MIKE: This is the best day of my fucking life!

KATIE: Now other fathers like Michael Chapman will be able to look forward to miracles.

JACK comes back.

JACK: Mike, Becky's a little agitated, I think she'd love to see you.

MIKE: What is it?

JACK: She's a little tearful. It's the thing about the cancer again. She seems to think I'd told her she had cancer.

MIKE exits, goes to BECKY.

Just hold her hand and reassure her. Tell her it's all going to be just fine.

[Interval.]

Scene 10

New York hospital: BECKY sleeping. MIKE wanders round the room, sings to himself.

MIKE: 'This is not the story of a pioneering doctor, this is the story of a father. Academy Award winner Tom Cruise is Mike Chapman. (*Tom Cruise voice.*) "Our family is a circle and that circle is never gonna be broken," a man prepared to sacrifice everything to save his beloved daughter. (*Tom Cruise voice.*) "I just want Becky to be well." Triple Academy Award-winner Robin Williams is Nobel Prize-winning doctor Jack Liebermann, the scientist they tried to silence: (*Robin Williams voice.*) "You can take away my professorship but you cannot hide the scientific truth." Together they think the unthinkable. Together they believe. (*Tom Cruise voice.*) "Just one more step Becky… Thank you God! God bless America!" '

BECKY gets out of bed, well, and comes up behind him. Sings 'Missing'.

He sings with her, doesn't look round.

BECKY: What about your love interest Dad? 'Double Academy Award winner Julia Roberts is Dr Cyndi Kitten, the physiotherapist with the very short skirt… (*Julia Roberts voice.*) "Mike, I'm scared, hold me." '

MIKE: Yeah, she takes off her glasses and shakes her hair down and goes, 'Oh Mike, you've never noticed me,' and I go, 'Yes I have but I was too shy.' It'll be really tastefully shot.

BECKY: I want a love interest an all.

MIKE: Yeah, there's a handsome junior doctor.

BECKY: Played by Johnny Depp.

MIKE: Yeah, played by Johnny Depp, and he takes pity on you and as a radical form of therapy he…

BECKY: Gives me one?

MIKE: Yeah.

BECKY: Does it work?

MIKE: No, but it makes him feel better.

BECKY: So I'm in bed, right, I'm dead ill. Shall I drool?

MIKE: Yeah.

BECKY: Nah, he won't fancy me if I'm drooling.

MIKE: You can start drooling when he comes in. (*Johnny Depp voice.*) Hello Becky.

BECKY: Doctor, are you really a doctor? You seem so out of place in this cold, clinical world.

MIKE: I'm only a junior doctor here, but I've thought of a radical new therapy…

MIKE turns into Robin Williams.

I am Dr Jack Liebermann, I have never lost a patient!

BECKY: Who's that meant to be?

MIKE: Robin Williams. Here, have this injection.

BECKY jumps up.

BECKY: Oh doctor, doctor, I feel different now and yet the same.

MIKE: Take the first step Becky, walk on your own.

MIKE / BECKY: Success!

KATIE appears.

BECKY returns to bed.

KATIE: The aggressive treatment programme that this horrific disease requires is an ordeal for Becky, already very sick. Ordinary daylight is now excruciatingly painful for her, she is constantly at the mercy of splitting headaches, and doctors are concerned that she may be beginning to lose the vision in her left eye. But her devoted father is undeterred.

KATIE holds out her Dictaphone to MIKE.

MIKE: It's hard for her, but she's got me with her.

KATIE: He told the *Post.*

MIKE: I told her I'd make her better and I won't go back on my word.

Scene 11

NY hospital, BECKY's room: BECKY sleeps. JACK enters, sits by BECKY's bed for a while looking at her. Takes her hand and checks her skin and fingernails, makes notes.

JACK: I'm trying to get your brain back, Becky, do you hear me? Don't let me down.

BECKY starts to cry.

Hey, hey.

JACK wipes BECKY's face with a damp cloth.

MIKE enters.

MIKE: She all right doc?

JACK: Yes Mike, just doing my checks.

MIKE: I think she's in less pain now. D'you reckon?

JACK: Yes, I'm sure.

MIKE: Still twitching a bit though. Didn't seem to make any difference, that thing you gave her.

JACK: It won't work immediately.

MIKE: Come on love, we're on the home straight now. We're killing the disease, I saw the scan. You've just got to stay strong till we get every last bit of it. You listening Becks?

BECKY throws up all over MIKE.

Oh, hey. Easy love. Shit, doc. There's blood. There's blood in it. That int good, is it? Vomiting blood. I don't know much but I know that int good.

JACK: Why don't you step into my office Mike? You'll find a fresh T shirt on the shelves by the door. Get yourself cleaned up and I'll be with you in just a moment.

MIKE: Nah, leave it, I'll do it later.

JACK: You need something to wear to get back to your hotel Mike. We don't want to frighten people do we?

MIKE doesn't move.

I'd like for us to have a chat, Mike, if that's convenient. I'll see you in my office in five minutes.

Scene 12

MIKE waiting in JACK's office. Dozes off. NIGHTMARE DOCTORS appear, reach out to shake his hand.

NIGHTMARE DOCTOR ONE: Hi Mr Chapman, it's really good to meet you.

NIGHTMARE DOCTOR 2 : We wanna offer you some wonderful cures. Way ahead of anything you could get in Britain.

NIGHTMARE DOCTOR ONE: We're gonna treat the disease in your daughter's brain in the most comfortable way possible. No drugs, no machines, no needles, my product is an air freshener. All she has to do is breathe.

NIGHTMARE DOCTOR TWO: In my laboratories we have formulated a drink. We have many different flavours; we could ask her what her favourite drink is and that is what her treatment would be.

NIGHTMARE DOCTOR ONE: She would get her speech back.

NIGHTMARE DOCTOR TWO: Does she play the violin?

MIKE shakes his head.

She'll be able to.

NIGHTMARE DOCTOR ONE: She'll be able to fly and do math like Albert Einstein.

NIGHTMARE DOCTOR TWO: She might be able to contact the dead.

NIGHTMARE DOCTOR ONE: The side effects are that it rots her intestines.

NIGHTMARE DOCTOR TWO: The side effects with the air freshener are that she grows three heads.

NIGHTMARE DOCTOR ONE: At least that's what happened with the mice.

They laugh maniacally.

NIGHTMARE DOCTOR TWO: But hey, three heads is very useful. When you're crossing the road one can look left, one can look right…

NIGHTMARE DOCTOR ONE: You do realise she'll grow fur?

NIGHTMARE DOCTOR TWO: She would become a small rabbit type thing.

NIGHTMARE DOCTOR ONE: Maybe an extra mammary gland, but maybe on her head.

NIGHTMARE DOCTOR TWO: At least that's what happened with the mice.

They laugh.

NIGHTMARE DOCTOR ONE: We could investigate a penis and vagina combo. She could have sex with herself.

NIGHTMARE DOCTOR TWO: Nobody else'd want to!

NIGHTMARE DOCTOR ONE: If you're gonna let us experiment on her we'd like to go the whole hog.

NIGHTMARE DOCTOR TWO: Literally.

They start to grunt. Then they start to make other animal noises: mooing, squeaking, monkey noises.

NIGHTMARE DOCTOR ONE: Sign here!

NIGHTMARE DOCTOR TWO: You've seen Dumbo, you believed the elephant could fly? Becky too! Just sign here!

They throw leaflets, samples, contracts to sign at him.

JACK enters. They disappear.

JACK: Mike. So sorry to keep you. Can I get you anything to drink?

Scene 13

ALAN's lab. CAROLINE waiting for ALAN. Tidying up his papers. ALAN enters.

ALAN: Got it. It was on the back seat under those Canadian papers. Must get round to them. Here you are.

CAROLINE: A Barbie cassette recorder?!

ALAN: It's got a good microphone. You have it in your pocket, you say the usual stuff at the meeting.

CAROLINE: That's all off the agenda now Alan.

ALAN: How can it be?

CAROLINE: We've got to look at sheep scrapie studies now and something about the age of slaughtered cows…

ALAN: You'll have to say it in any other business then. It's not off the agenda is it? It can't just be off the agenda…

CAROLINE: Alan…

ALAN: You say something, and they won't minute it and you can get hold of the minutes. And we give that to the press, with the tape, show them how they're ignoring us.

CAROLINE: All that's just politics. We need to concentrate on what we know about and try to get the evidence…

ALAN: I can't concentrate on what I know about!

CAROLINE: Gosh, I'm so sorry. You must be devastated about your funding.

ALAN: Yes. Especially as it came so quickly after the sudden 'membership review' of the SDIC and surprise, surprise, no room for me…

CAROLINE: They have treated you appallingly.

ALAN: It's not just that. They've cancelled my lab account and they've got me under surveillance. They're probably watching you too. Have you noticed anything funny?

CAROLINE: No.

ALAN: How's the research going?

CAROLINE: I got some leads from your friend with the support group. But I'm waiting for the neuropath again. It seems to be taking...

ALAN: It seems to be taking longer than usual? You see! They're trying to stop us Caroline!

CAROLINE: You're getting all... Is this about them? That girl, and this woman, Karen?

ALAN: No! It's about the hypocrisy...

CAROLINE: You only get like this when you go out of your lab and mix yourself up in other people's emotions, because you don't know how to...

ALAN: Spare me the pop psychology!

CAROLINE: You know I'm right.

ALAN: Are you going to help me?

CAROLINE: I can't.

ALAN: Why not?

CAROLINE: I'm thinking of standing down from the SDIC anyway.

ALAN: What?

CAROLINE: I need to get on with finding more cases and get this paper finished. And I want them to take it seriously when I do. I don't want them to dismiss it because...

ALAN: Because they think you're a trouble maker? Better stay in with the big boys, better not rock the boat...

CAROLINE: Shut up and listen to me Alan. When we publish this I think they're going to have to admit it.

Scene 14

New York Hospital. JACK's office. Darkness. MIKE going through JACK's papers. JACK enters, switches the light on.

JACK: Mr Chapman. What are you looking for?

MIKE: I just want to know what else you've got. There must be other stuff. What about other doctors? What do they think? There's other stuff you're not telling me about int there?

JACK: You have no authorisation...

MIKE: I know the quinacrine's your big thing and you might not want to admit it if you've got it wrong, but that don't matter. We can just...

JACK: You saw the scan Mike. The quinacrine gets to the abnormal prions in the brain.

MIKE: Yeah, but she int just a brain is she? That's the problem with you – everyone's just a test tube on legs.

JACK: This was made clear to you when we started treatment Mike. The problem we have is that anything powerful enough to destroy the abnormal prions is also going to have an effect on other organs of the body.

MIKE: Yeah, too much for her to handle and you knew that dint you? But you just wanted to have a look what happened...

JACK: And you've seen what happened! You saw her improve! With any challenging disease like this one someone has to be the first...

MIKE: Yeah, maybe. But I don't want it to be me!

JACK: It's a pity you feel that way because I think you and Becky are both being very courageous and I'm very grateful...

MIKE: Yeah cause now you know that it fucks with her liver and you probably knew that all along dint you? What happened to your mice, eh?

JACK: If you're going to get aggressive I'm afraid I'll have to call security.

MIKE: What happened to the fucking mice?

MIKE pins JACK against the wall.

JACK presses a button and the security alarm goes off.

Music: MIKE and BECKY singing 'They Can't Take That Away From Me.'

End of Act Two.

ACT THREE

Scene 1

Pub: MIKE's comedy routine.

MIKE: (*Singing.*) That's the wonder, the wonder of you…
Thank you very much indeed ladies and gentlemen. The
King. Haven't got to Memphis yet. New York's
something though, int it?

Our Becky weren't too well, that's why I had to take her
to the States for treatment. She fell over in Morrisons so
I took her to the GP for some tests. We went back a few
weeks later and he said he had good news and bad news.
I asked what the good news was and he said she'd be
famous as the first person to die of mad cow disease. He
told me that this mad cow thing happens when human
protein gets crossed with cow protein. I told him the
mother-in-law had once tried to have sex with a bull and
he asked what happened so I said nowt, you know there
are some things even a bull won't do.

He said the bad news was that our Becky would
gradually lose motor function. I said she hadn't even
started her driving lessons yet but he said he meant she'd
lose control of her limbs, which were why she'd fallen
over in Morrisons. I said no, that were because she'd had
three packets of Cheesy Wotsits and a Muller Fruit
Corner down her knickers and she'd been trying to get
out without security spotting her when the Muller had
fallen out and she'd slipped in the resulting mess. He
disagreed and said she were showing all the signs of
nvCJD. I said she never wears anything but FCUK and
if she'd worn proper knickers instead of a thong, we
wouldn't be here now.

That were that really, the next time we saw the doctor he said he didn't think she had long left. I asked him how long and he said, 'Ten.' I said ten what? Months, weeks, what? He said, 'Nine.'

Scene 2

MIKE's house: CHARLIE and KAREN watching TV.

CHARLIE: I don't want to stay at nan's again.

KAREN: We've been through this Charlie. I've got important things to do.

CHARLIE coughs.

CHARLIE: I don't think I'm very well.

KAREN: Oh dear.

CHARLIE: Can you turn the sound down on the telly? Auntie Karen? It's too noisy.

KAREN: Don't be daft.

CHARLIE: It's really loud Auntie Karen, it hurts my head. I need some tablets. I need a glass of water.

KAREN: Have you lost the use of your legs an' all?

CHARLIE: Yeah, I think so. Can I lie on the sofa? Can you turn the light off?

KAREN: You'd better go up to bed love if you're that sick. Alan's coming round. We'll be talking.

CHARLIE: What about?

KAREN: About Becky, and the government.

CHARLIE: You're always talking about Becky and the government.

The doorbell rings.

KAREN: Upstairs.

KAREN lets ALAN in.

ALAN: Hello Charlie.

CHARLIE: I can't walk. Look.

Gets up, tries to walk, falls over.

KAREN: Have you got any idea how boring this is Charlie? We've just been through months of this for real.

CHARLIE: (*Crying.*) I might die!

KAREN: You 'ant got it!

CHARLIE: I have got it! You just don't believe me cause you never listen to me!

ALAN: Oh dear. That looks very serious. Take a seat Charlie. I need to do an important test.

He opens his bag and rummages around.

Now. Can you try to answer this question for me?

CHARLIE: Yes.

ALAN: Do you want a Mars bar?

CHARLIE: Yes.

ALAN: Then I declare you well.

He gives her a Mars bar.

KAREN: Now go and watch your telly upstairs.

CHARLIE runs off.

She's been driving me mad.

ALAN: She's upset.

KAREN: You're good with kids.

ALAN: They remind me of scientists.

KAREN: You never told me you and Caroline used to...

ALAN: It was years ago. She left me for a very successful idiot.

MIKE enters, pushing BECKY in a wheelchair. BECKY smiles but is sleepy and unresponsive.

MIKE: We're home! Anyone here?

They walk in.

KAREN runs to greet them.

KAREN: Oh my God! What are you doing here?

KAREN hugs BECKY.

How are you love? How is she? She looks...

MIKE: She's just a bit knackered, that's all.

KAREN and MIKE hug.

KAREN: You look knackered an' all.

MIKE: Just jetlag.

KAREN: What's happened Mike?

MIKE: Hey, hey, nowt's happened. Aren't you going to introduce me? Sorry if we interrupted summat here.

KAREN: Don't be daft Mike. This is Alan. I told you, the doctor.

They shake hands.

MIKE: Nice to meet you mate. 'Scuse us barging in, it's just that Becky's really been wanting to come home, 'ant you love? And finally they said she could so we got the next flight.

ALAN: What about the treatment?

MIKE: Yeah, it's all looking good.

CHARLIE comes downstairs.

CHARLIE: Dad!

MIKE hugs CHARLIE.

Is Becky better?

CHARLIE goes to BECKY.

Why's she all yellow?

MIKE: Cause she's my lemon princess.

KAREN: I think we should put Becky to bed.

CHARLIE: What's a lemon princess?

MIKE: I 'ant got the energy to get her up the stairs right now.

ALAN: Do you want some help?

MIKE: D'you mind mate?

ALAN and MIKE take BECKY up the stairs and put her to bed.

Liebermann knows what he's doing.

ALAN: Good.

MIKE: You don't rate him do you?

ALAN: Yes I do but he…none of us have all the answers.

MIKE: Thanks for all the…advice and stuff you've been giving Karen. Thing is, I don't want her getting worried. She panics. Anything you think about Becky…let's keep it between me and you, eh?

ALAN: All right.

MIKE: I tell you what, I 'ant seen Karen with a new hair cut for three years, and she works in a hairdressers. And she's got a bit of make up on an' all. You've made quite an impression.

ALAN: Oh no, it's not like that.

MIKE: It might not be to you but I know our Karen. I don't want anyone pissing her around.

ALAN: I won't be doing that Mike. It's nice to meet you. I'll leave you in peace now.

ALAN says his goodbyes and exits.

MIKE: (*To CHARLIE.*) Bed time now love. You'll get your presents in the morning.

CHARLIE goes upstairs to BECKY's room.

KAREN: What's going on?

MIKE: Nowt. We had a nice chat. He's a good bloke. Just don't get your hopes up too much love cause I think his interest's purely professional.

KAREN: I won't talking about Alan. What's going on with Becky?

MIKE: We're home to see you, for a nice surprise.

KAREN: How come they let you back home?

MIKE: Cause they said she's well enough to travel, so I've got all the pills she needs and we've just got to go back in a couple of weeks.

KAREN: You didn't say owt about that before. Tell me exactly what they said Mike.

MIKE: Hey, we'll talk tomorrow. I'm knackered.

KAREN: I can see that. You look like you 'ant slept for weeks. I don't know if you know what's real and what int anymore.

MIKE: I'm fine Karen.

KAREN: Mike, listen to me. Promise me you won't get upset.

MIKE: What, even if you punch me in the face?

KAREN: You're always joking.

MIKE: You love me, though, don't you?

KAREN: I know all about the quinacrine. I know the reason they don't use it in this country.

MIKE: Because they don't sell it.

KAREN: Because it affects the liver.

MIKE: Yeah but it's OK cause there's stuff they can do for that. We've got all sorts of things for her to take and in the end, if they need to, they can give her a bit of dialysis.

KAREN: And the other things have side effects and then they pump her with more things for them side effects…

MIKE: It's just till we get enough quinacrine in there to kill the bad cells. We're nearly there Karen.

KAREN: It's an endless cycle of suffering!

MIKE: Don't say I'm making her suffer. That int fair. You'd just let her down would you?

KAREN: Yes. Gently.

MIKE: She's gonna get better!

KAREN: It's a terminal disease!

MIKE: Who told you that?

KAREN: Alan gave me scientific reports and I read them all Mike.

MIKE: Alan told me himself nobody knows. They all hate Liebermann because they're jealous.

KAREN: Don't take her back there, Mike.

MIKE: You're just like the rest of them. I can't believe I'm hearing this from you. Liebermann's working on new stuff, he's working on a way of getting the quinacrine straight into the brain, so it don't have to go near the liver. He think's it'll be ready in four weeks. We can't give up now. Karen, come on, don't let me down.

KAREN starts to cry.

Hey, don't do that. Come here, wipe your eyes. I think there's a non-snotty corner on there somewhere.

KAREN: It's not fair on Charlie, Mike.

MIKE: I'll talk to her.

KAREN: Please don't lie to her. You've got to stop lying...

MIKE: All right, all right. I'm not lying. Well, I might have lied about there being a non-snotty bit on that tissue.

Scene 3

CHARLIE in BECKY's room. BECKY in bed.

CHARLIE: I'm glad you came back cause Auntie Karen's doing a campaign to tell the government what to do and I was going to have to stay with nan and make conversation.

Auntie Karen were getting worried that you were never coming back cause she said Dad had had a nervous breakdown. Sounds like a car.

Dad said the doctors in America are making you better but it don't look like it.

It's OK though cause Alan can make you better. He can put daisies in your head.

Dad says you're yellow cause you're a lemon princess. Why's Dad keep saying so much stupid stuff? I think it's embarrassing. I'm not being mean but I don't reckon you look like a princess. I reckon you look more like a big canary, like that canary nan had that used to peck Dad's head.

BECKY laughs very weakly.

Listen.

CHARLIE plays the dictaphone tape of BECKY and CHARLIE singing 'All I Wanna Do.'

BECKY leans over the bed and vomits.

CHARLIE jumps up.

CHARLIE: Ugh.

BECKY stays where she was, too weak to move back.

CHARLIE stares at her.

Scene 4

MIKE's house: BECKY's room. BECKY sleeping. Moonlight. MIKE comes in.

MIKE: All right love? Could've sworn you shouted summat.

He feels her forehead, rearranges her covers etc.

You're OK then.

Bugger me. It's Jesus. It's bloody Jesus all bloody shining. What d'you reckon to that love? He's looking after you. You know what that means? It's a sign. You're going to be OK. I know it. You've just got to trust me.

I know your Auntie Karen don't believe it, lots of people don't believe it, but I know we're gonna do it. Jesus is with us. Look.

Yeah, yeah, I know it's Ryan Giggs. But still. I swear it really looked like Jesus there with the moon on it.

I know, I know. I think your Auntie Karen thinks I'm mad an' all. Thing is she just don't get it. What we have to do. I'm thinking totally clear.

Just tried Jack but he int available. But I'll try again tomorrow. I'm not gonna let you down Becks.

Scene 5

MIKE's house. CHARLIE arrives home from school.

CHARLIE: Dad!

MIKE shouts from the next room.

MIKE: Just a second love. Good day at school?

CHARLIE: No.

MIKE: Eh?

CHARLIE: Dad? It says in the paper the doctors in America can't make our Becky better.

MIKE comes in. Blood on his clothes and hands.

MIKE: You don't want to pay any attention to things you see in the paper Charlie.

CHARLIE: But everyone said it. And they called me a mad cow and they said I'm mooing and no one can touch me cause they'll catch –

She notices the blood.

What've you done Dad?!

MIKE: Shhh, it's nowt.

CHARLIE: Have you cut yourself?

MIKE: No, it's our Becky. It's OK. I'll just get her cleaned up.

CHARLIE: Can I see her?

MIKE: No love. Put the telly on, that's a good girl. I'll be with you in a minute.

He exits.

CHARLIE starts to cry.

MIKE comes back.

CHARLIE: Has Becky died?

MIKE: No, no. She int even hurt.

CHARLIE: That int true.

MIKE: It is love.

CHARLIE: I'm not a baby Dad, you can't tell me she int hurt when I can see the blood!

MIKE: OK, listen to me. Did your Auntie Karen or your big sister…did they ever tell you about periods? Or at school maybe…? No? Well…thing is, I'm not really the best person to… Best thing is, if you ask your Auntie Karen to tell you about it, OK? Cause it's a special thing that women know about. Our Becky's fine. I just forgot this month to give her the pills that stop it, that's all.

CHARLIE: She's going to be OK?

MIKE: Yes love, she's fine.

He hugs her. Starts to fall asleep.

CHARLIE: Dad?

MIKE: Hmmm?

CHARLIE: Today at school…

MIKE: Tell me later. I just need to shut my eyes for five minutes while our Becky's sleeping. Watch your programmes in your room till tea time.

Scene 6

MIKE's house. CHARLIE playing. KATIE enters

KATIE: Oh, hello Charlie darling. Where's your Dad?

CHARLIE shrugs.

KATIE sits on the floor with CHARLIE.

It's quite hard to get hold of him these days. And your Auntie Karen. I think they're very busy aren't they?

CHARLIE: Yeah. Cause of our Becky.

KATIE squeezes CHARLEY's hand.

KATIE: I think you're being a really big, brave girl Charlie. You must be really missing having your sister to play with.

CHARLIE: 'And I miss you, like the deserts in the rain.' That's what she used to sing.

KATIE: That's lovely.

CHARLIE: She can't say stuff now. It's like after grandad's stroke, she talks out the corner of her mouth. And she can't go to the toilet by herself. Dad has to wash her and he sings stupid songs to her like she's a little kid or summat.

Dad thinks I don't know but I know she's really, really poorly.

KATIE: It's so difficult isn't it Charlie? You feel so helpless seeing someone ill.

CHARLIE: I think Auntie Karen thinks Becky's going to die cause she cries all the time. Last night Dad lay down on the sofa with Becky and he said I wish the disease would go out of her head and into my head and Auntie Karen cried. I saw them.

KATIE: I know just what you're going through sweetheart. I was in tears all the time when we were all in America. Cause it was so hard seeing how sick she was. But you know what you have to do? You have to try as hard as you can to be positive. That means look for the good things.

CHARLIE: Dad says that an' all but I don't know what they are.

KATIE: Well I think maybe one thing we can do is that if we tell Becky's story lots of other people will be able to understand. Do you know what I'm interested in now Charlie? I'm interested in whose fault it might be that Becky got ill and whether we can make them say sorry. Do you know why Becky got ill?

CHARLIE: Cause of eating beefburgers.

KATIE: How do you know that?

CHARLIE: Auntie Karen and Alan told me. You know when you saw the cows on the telly falling over? That's what our Becky were like at the beginning when she used to fall over, cause it's the same disease the cows had. What happens is, if you eat cows that have eaten other cows then your brain turns into a cow's brain and you turn like a mad cow. But I'm not allowed to say mad cow about our Becky, and once when she was cross and I called her a mardy cow Dad said I couldn't have a Twix in my lunch for a week. At school they play mad cows in the playground, where you run and if the mad cow touches you you have to fall over. And I get teased sometimes.

Auntie Karen threw out all the burgers and she's a vegetarian now. I want to be a vegetarian but I don't like vegetables.

Auntie Karen says it's David Seaman Gumtree's fault. That's a man.

KATIE reading her report.

KATIE: This family are convinced that the government are hiding the truth from the victims of this terrible disease. The *Post* has pledged to get to the bottom of the scandal of BSE beef and CJD. Watch this space for exclusive evidence from an eminent British scientist. After you've read this you'll never eat a beefburger again.

Scene 7

The Inquiry.

CHAIR: Did you have specific guidance from the Prime Minister about your role regarding scientific research into CJD?

HEALTH MINISTER: I really don't recall...

CHAIR: This memo sent to you by the Prime Minister on 8th April 1996 might remind you. Read it to us please.

HEALTH MINISTER: 'It would be desirable for the Health Ministry to do everything in its power to delay publication of any scientific research which suggests a link between BSE and CJD until after press coverage of the European bans has abated and if at all possible until after the election.'

CHAIR: Is it correct, Minister, that you asked one of your civil servants to monitor the activities of Dr Harding and Dr Andrews?

HEALTH MINISTER: Yes, according to instructions from the Prime Minister.

CHAIR: Did the Prime Minister tell you to restrict their access to research materials?

HEALTH MINISTER: Not in so many words but I was supposed to delay their research. All that I was doing was following instructions from my superiors…

CHAIR: And after the article in the *Daily Post* on 18th June 1996, suggesting that scientists suspected a link between BSE and CJD, what were your instructions then?

HEALTH MINISTER: I was told to keep the scientists quiet.

CHAIR: Were those the words the Prime Minister used?

HEALTH MINISTER: No. Actually he said 'shut them up'. And then he told me I had to 'do something to show Dr Andrews who's boss'. All right?

Scene 8

ALAN's lab. Late at night. ALAN working. MIKE enters.

MIKE: Glad you're here. Sorry it's so late. Just she wouldn't stop throwing up and I had to wait for it to calm down.

ALAN: Did we arrange...?

MIKE: No, we didn't arrange owt. But then I never arranged to be at me daughter's bedside holding her head up while she pukes her guts out and cries and trying to understand what she wants cause she can't speak no more.

She can't speak Alan. She's seventeen.

ALAN: Sit down Mike.

MIKE doesn't sit.

MIKE: So what's this thing Charlie's going on about with daisies? That's not serious is it? Cause if I took our Becks to New York for however many millions of dollars' worth of treatment and she could've got the same thing from going over the rec and eating some daisies, I'm gonna feel like a bit of a pillock.

ALAN: It is serious. There's a chemical in daisy leaves that might be useful...

MIKE: That's smart, cause they probably don't have side effects, do they, daisies?

ALAN: Did Dr Liebermann say the side effects of the quinacrine...?

MIKE: That stuff really works, don't it, on the brain damage? It's amazing. I saw a scan.

ALAN: Yes.

MIKE: D'you know about this quinacrine they can get straight into the brain? Are you working on that an' all?

ALAN: Not with quinacrine, but the idea of getting drugs to the brain...

MIKE: Liebermann said four weeks but there's been some sort of hold up. It's just that every week counts for us, you know, at the moment.

ALAN: Mike, I don't really understand why Dr
Liebermann...

MIKE: What else are you working on, apart from the
daisies? Karen said you've got loads of ideas.

ALAN: Some different anti-oxidants, things called COX-2
inhibitors and peptidase inhibitors.

MIKE: Sounds like good stuff. If you've got anything you
want to try then I say let's just go for it. What have we
got to lose, eh?

ALAN: Mike, have you been to your GP, to the hospital?

MIKE: Course I have but they 'ant got a clue have they?
They just go on about making her comfortable. I need
someone with vision. You're working on the stuff they're
going to be using for this in five years or whatever.
Thing is our Becks needs it now.

ALAN: I can't just start a programme of treatment on
someone...

MIKE: Just think, she could be the first one to recover from
this and then you'd get your funding and everything
wouldn't you?

ALAN: Mike, please. Will you just sit down for a minute?
We need to...

MIKE: Yeah, all right, but can I just go and get Becks, cause
she's out in the car.

ALAN: You brought her here?

MIKE: Yeah, cause it's pretty urgent, you know? We need to
start some sort of treatment...

Now.

Please.

Scene 9

Government office: HEALTH MINISTER, ALAN, CAROLINE.
HEALTH MINISTER throws a copy of the Daily Post *on the table*
in front of them.

HEALTH MINISTER: My colleagues and I were…well, I
don't think I'd be exaggerating if I said we were
astonished to see that you've decided to link yourselves
with the gutter press. The 'eminent scientist' here refers
to you I take it Dr Andrews. I didn't think you had much
respect for publications like the *Daily Post.*

ALAN: I don't.

HEALTH MINISTER: Come on. Everyone knows your
connection with this family.

ALAN: Why does everyone know? I'm just trying to get on
with my job and I don't understand why people are
spying on me.

HEALTH MINISTER: No one is spying on you, but these
are important issues and you are an expert in your field,
so naturally it matters to the government what you say
to the press. And Dr Harding, for a member of the SDIC
to be linked to an article in which an entirely unqualified
hairdresser from Leeds makes unsubstantiated assertions
about CJD and beef is…well, it's not exactly professional
is it?

CAROLINE: I wouldn't have to look for cases through the
press if you funded me properly.

HEALTH MINISTER: So now that you're working in
partnership with the *Daily Post,* have you been deluged
by calls from people under 45 with CJD?

CAROLINE: I've found two more interesting cases through
the article.

HEALTH MINISTER: And how many people have you had phoning up saying, 'I keep losing my keys. Have I got CJD?'

CAROLINE: I have had a call from the *Guardian* and one from *The Times*.

HEALTH MINISTER: I do need to make it clear, Dr Harding, that for a member of the SDIC to talk to the press about...

CAROLINE: I gave my resignation letter to the Chairman of the SDIC today.

HEALTH MINISTER: I see. That's a great pity. I hope you will reconsider that decision.

CAROLINE: No thank you. I've got my research to do.

HEALTH MINISTER: Even so, your unit is funded with government money isn't it Dr Harding? The government and its advisors are going to make a balanced decision about which statements we make to the public at which times. And if other scientists seek to try to get attention and glory for themselves by telling stories to the press then...

CAROLINE: You'll take their funding away?

HEALTH MINISTER: I didn't say that.

ALAN: You're not funding me any more so what have I got to lose if I talk to them?

HEALTH MINISTER: Perhaps a reason we might not be keen to fund your work, Dr Andrews, is because we have some concerns about the tone in which you talk about this subject, a tone which, if you were to use it to speak to the press...

ALAN: Then what?

HEALTH MINISTER: I think it would be a very bad decision for your career and could make your life quite difficult if you were to talk to the press about this.

ALAN: Are you threatening me?

HEALTH MINISTER: Don't be ridiculous. I'm simply explaining that if you were to speak to them in this way we might feel that your approach was in conflict with the government's feeling about the issue. If, on the other hand, you were able to be a little more balanced in the statements you made then we might...

ALAN: Give me my funding back?

HEALTH MINISTER: It's possible.

ALAN: As long as I don't talk to the press.

HEALTH MINISTER: Yes.

ALAN: Thank you.

Scene 10

MIKE's house. MIKE sleeping on the sofa. Starts to dream. CHARLIE comes in.

CHARLIE: Dad, I had a bad dream.

MIKE: You know monsters don't really exist don't you?

CHARLIE: It were about our Becky. She were playing with the dolphins and she couldn't swim no more and she fell to the bottom and drowned.

MIKE: Well, you know how dreams work? How they work is that whatever happens in dreams, the exact opposite happens in real life.

CHARLIE: You mean she can swim?

MIKE: She's going to be fine.

CHARLIE: She's not going to die like Mam?

MIKE: Why're you asking all these questions? Don't you believe me?

CHARLIE: Which one is it? Is she or int she?

Pause. MIKE takes a deep breath.

MIKE: The situation is that the treatment might not've worked so we've got to face up to the fact that she's going to be absolutely fine, and it might be soon. They'll take her off the drugs and then she'll be fine.

CHARLIE: So she'll get better then?

MIKE: She's gonna die. She's just getting worse and worse. We saw the brain scan and the black bit's getting bigger and bigger. It was great, the doctors said get up, you can walk, and she doesn't, she falls over like a cow!

CHARLIE: I don't want our Becky to die. I want you to die instead.

MIKE: Me too love.

Well BECKY enters.

BECKY: It hurt. All the time.

CHARLIE: He lied to me.

BECKY: He lied to everybody. 'Lie to me…' (*She sings the chorus from 'Strong Enough'.*)

CHARLIE: Let's get rid of Dad and have Mum and Becky back.

BECKY: Two for one, like you get in Morrisons.

MIKE: Well I'll go on the Internet tomorrow and sort it out with God. You can find it all on the search engine.

BECKY: And don't forget to get the journalists round to film it Dad.

MIKE thrashes in his sleep.

Scene 11

ALAN's lab: ALAN comes in. KATIE is snooping around.

ALAN: Can I help you?

KATIE: Katie Conway, *Daily Post.* It was open.

ALAN: What do you want?

KATIE: There's a girl dying Dr Andrews. Becky Chapman. I think you know her. I think she's dying because she ate infected beef and I think the government owes the people of this country an explanation. Would you be prepared to talk to the *Post...*?

ALAN: Isn't it a bit late to ask me when you've already told your readers I'm going to?

KATIE: Oh but I was sure you would. Because it's such a scandal isn't it?

KATIE sees empty cages.

Gosh, it is true that you let your mice go?

ALAN: What?

KATIE: I really only need a few words, Dr...

ALAN: Did you talk to that kid?

KATIE: What?

ALAN: You talked to Charlie didn't you? That's where you got that stuff about me! I can't believe you people!

KATIE: It's not like that Dr Andrews...

ALAN: You're exploiting people's suffering.

KATIE: (*Hurt.*) That's not fair! The *Post*'s been setting the agenda with this story! Just because I make it accessible to ordinary people doesn't mean I'm exploiting them. I've been through so much with that family. And I think we owe it to Mike to keep fighting! That man's broken, he's given everything for his daughter...

ALAN: I've read what you've been writing. It's sensationalist, inaccurate drivel.

The lights go out. It is very dark. Noise of someone coming into the lab.

Who's that?

Someone grabs KATIE. She yelps, struggles, escapes and runs away.

What are...?

Sound of a scuffle, ALAN cries out in pain. Then is knocked to the floor. Torchlight. The intruder turning the lab upside down.

KATIE in a spot, breathless and dishevelled, one shoe missing.

KATIE: There's been a shocking new twist to the increasingly sordid affair of the government's attempt to cover up scientists' concerns about the safety of British beef. Late last night in an isolated area on the outskirts of Leeds, this reporter watched as the scientist who was poised to tell the *Post* his story was prevented from doing so by the forced intrusion of a masked figure to his laboratory. Was this man working for the government? Is this just the tip of a terrible and shameful iceberg?

Scene 12

MIKE's house. MIKE sleeping on the sofa. KAREN enters.

KAREN: Have you heard about Alan?

MIKE: Eh?

KAREN: They went after Alan, someone from the government or summat. And they don't know where he is. What d'you think they've done to him? I don't know what they'd do...

MIKE: Hey, hey, it'll be fine.

KAREN notices CHARLEY's Barbie dictaphone on the table.

KAREN: What's that doing there?

MIKE: That's our Charlie's int it?

KAREN: But what's it doing back here?

She picks it up, checks inside it for the tape.

MIKE: I brought it back from Alan's the other day. She must've left it there.

KAREN: What were you doing at Alan's?

MIKE: Just went to have a chat with him. About his daisies.

KAREN: Why didn't you tell me?

MIKE: Karen, love...

KAREN: Tell me the truth Mike!

MIKE: I just went to ask Alan about his daisies...

KAREN: Mike, for once in your life tell me the fucking truth!

MIKE: Calm down. All right, all right.

He sighs.

I don't know where to start.

KAREN: Start from the bit where you stopped telling me what's going on with Becky.

MIKE: All right. I don't know how to say this… We had enough money, I was gonna stay, but then he came in, Jack…

He came in and said how are you, d'you want a drink and stuff, they were always saying stuff like that, they were so… He showed me some results. Of the liver scans. It could've been fucking Chinese. I said looks OK to me and he said *Oh.* I said what's that *Oh* mean? Don't sound very good. He said ten more days of treatment and I just sat there thinking ten days to get better, that's what I heard. He didn't explain it. You don't want to seem like you're thick do you? Sorry doc, can you give me the Ladybird Book of Science version? I said OK we'll go home for a bit and then come back, and he said no you won't, they won't give her no more. We have to suspend treatment he said.

I tried to nick some to bring it home. They caught me at it. Started going on at me about talking to a shrink.

You were right all along and I were wrong. I'm sorry.

So she's off it now, she's not on owt now. But I don't want to give up Karen. I promised her. So I was talking to Alan about whether he had owt, whether he had any quinacrine…

KAREN: Mike…

MIKE: Thing is she's my daughter. And she int dead yet! She's still alive! If I just say, 'Oh I'll not bother now,' how am I gonna feel for the rest of me life?

KAREN: Do you know where Alan is Mike?

MIKE: No I don't know, and I don't fucking care! It's my daughter I care about, I care about getting her better and everyone's treating me like I've lost it or summat cause I want my daughter to live!

KAREN: You have lost it Mike. If you were thinking straight you'd know that Becky would want you to stop now, to let her…

MIKE: You don't know that! Have you asked her? No you 'ant, cause you can't. But I'm her Dad! And I know the thing I've got to do is I've got to get her to keep fighting, and then maybe…

KAREN: She'll recover from a disease there's no cure for? Mike, you've got to…

MIKE: Everyone has to tell me what to do and I'm her Dad, no fucker else is her Dad. You're telling me what to do all the fucking time!

He throws a chair.

I just want somebody on my side!

Now see what you've done, I've bust me best fucking chair 'ant I?

You see them growing up don't you? You see them doing all the things they do.

KAREN: Oh for fuck's sake Michael. Why's it always about you? Why int it about Becky?

MIKE: It is about Becky!

KAREN: Becky's gone! She don't even know who we are anymore! She don't know you're her Dad!

You're never gonna get Becky back, Mike. She's gone.

Scene 13

The Inquiry.

CHAIR: You finally made your statement announcing a possible link between BSE and CJD on June 23rd 1996. What was it that made you announce this when you did?

HEALTH MINISTER: The article in the *Lancet* by staff at the CJD Surveillance Unit had persuaded our advisers that there was a…shift in the balance of probabilities, so…

CHAIR: So when they communicated this opinion to you, you immediately agreed to make the statement?

HEALTH MINISTER: The Prime Minister asked me to make a judgement about whether that would be necessary.

CHAIR: And your view was?

HEALTH MINISTER: I…

CHAIR: Perhaps the memo speaks for itself, Minister.

HEALTH MINISTER: 'This might be a desirable time to create a temporary distraction for the media to give us time to gather dissenting views from scientists to dilute the impact of the announcement.'

CHAIR: You changed your mind on June 21st though, Minister.

HEALTH MINISTER: I talked to the scientists again.

CHAIR: Looking for your dissenting views?

HEALTH MINISTER: Actually they asked to see me.

CHAIR: Who specifically?

HEALTH MINISTER: I had a visit from the Chairman of the Royal Society.

CHAIR: And your next memo?

HEALTH MINISTER: 'The Royal Society has made it clear that it will support any scientist who speaks out on this subject, and has indicated that the weight of scientific opinion, both here and abroad, supports the conclusions of the *Lancet* Report. I therefore believe that it will no longer be possible to conceal this information from the public.'

Scene 14

MIKE's house. BECKY on the sofa, the family sit around her.

CHARLIE: Dad, are we gonna give her another drink from that tube?

MIKE: No love.

KAREN: You can just keep her lips wet with a little bit of water, look, like this.

MIKE: Charlie, you'll have to say bye to your big sister soon.

CHARLIE: Why, are you going back to America?

KAREN: No.

CHARLIE: Where's she going then?

KAREN: She's going where your Mum went. Up to heaven with the angels.

CHARLIE: No she int! That's stupid. You said we could look after her and make her better.

KAREN: We tried, love, but it didn't work.

CHARLIE: But we can keep trying. I don't mind looking after her. She can come and live with me when I'm grown up.

KAREN: There's nowt we can do love. Not even the doctors can do owt now.

CHARLIE: But you said if we helped her she'd get better! You said Dad!

KAREN: Shhh, Charlie. We just didn't know. Be nice and quiet now. You can't keep your eyes open Mike. Go and lie down.

MIKE: No.

CHARLIE: Dad, you said Mum wouldn't die too but she did.

KAREN: Shhh.

CHARLIE: Mum had long hair.

KAREN takes CHARLIE away.

MIKE: Just let yourself go now love.

Pause.

BECKY gets up slowly, her cover falls to the ground.

MIKE picks it up and holds it.

BECKY makes the change to become the CHAIR in the Inquiry.

MIKE slowly follows her and makes the change to become the HEALTH MINISTER.

Scene 15

The Inquiry.

CHAIR: There were calls for your resignation, Minister, when the link between BSE and CJD was finally announced. You didn't resign at this point did you?

HEALTH MINISTER: No.

CHAIR: At what point did you resign?

HEALTH MINISTER: When the press started a campaign alleging the government was responsible for an assault on Dr Andrews...allegations which are still not substantiated.

CHAIR: Not quite the distracting story you'd been planning was it?

Picks up the Barbie dictaphone, removes tape from it.

Miss Conway, is this the tape you were given, a transcript of which was published in the *Daily Post* on June 27th 1996?

KATIE: Yes.

CHAIR: Where did this tape come from?

KATIE: It was brought to me by Karen Richardson, a friend of Dr Andrews.

CHAIR: Let's hear a section of the tape.

We hear the voices of ALAN and HEALTH MINISTER on the tape:

HEALTH MINISTER: I think it would be a very bad decision for your career and could make your life quite difficult if you were to talk to the press about this.

ALAN: Are you threatening me?

HEALTH MINISTER: Don't be ridiculous. I'm simply explaining that if you were to speak to them in this way we might feel that your approach was in conflict with the government's feeling about the issue. If, on the other hand, you were able to be a little more balanced in the statements you made, then we might...

ALAN: Give me my funding back?

HEALTH MINISTER: It's possible.

ALAN: As long as I don't talk to the press.

HEALTH MINISTER: Yes.

CHAIR: That is you speaking Minister?

HEALTH MINISTER: Yes, this has been flogged to death. And I absolutely deny that I had anything to do with Dr Andrews running away!

Scene 16

MIKE's house. MIKE and CHARLIE. MIKE sits on the sofa motionless. CHARLIE playing, making her toys talk.

CHARLIE:

Toy Cow: We are here today because of the tragic death of Lucy the ballerina who fell from the windowsill and lost the elastic holding her leg. She were the best dancer and also the most beautiful ballerina cause of her golden hair.

Barbie 2: It don't feel like Lucy's in that box. It just feels like she's away somewhere else.

Toy Cow: We will now sing 'All I wanna do is have some fun'.

CHARLIE sings the song.

Barbie 1: Lucy's in heaven now. She wanted to go away and be with Jesus. And all the famous people that are in heaven.

Barbie 2: Only babies think that. There's no such thing as heaven. Lucy's in the ground with creepy crawlies all over her.

Toy Cow: No fighting in the church! Now everyone has to say something good that Lucy did.

Barbie 1: Lucy were so kind. She always let me wear the red tutu even though it were the one she came in.

Barbie 2: She were my only sister.

We used to listen to music and make up dances and now I have to do it by myself. I feel sad that she int here no more, cause she were my big sister and now I don't have a big sister no more.

I want her to come back.

She used to play with my hair.

CHARLIE cries.

KAREN comes in. Goes to CHARLIE and hugs her.

KAREN: There there love. Be big and strong. Becky wouldn't want us all sad would she? Go and give your Dad a hug.

CHARLIE hesitates.

Mike?

MIKE looks at them.

Charlie needs a hug.

Go on pet. I'll make some tea.

CHARLIE goes to MIKE and sits with him. He puts his arm round her but is still distracted. CHARLIE buries her face in him.

KAREN comes back.

There's no milk left.

MIKE: I've had about fifty cups of tea today.

KAREN: I know. I brought you a beer instead.

MIKE: That's more like it.

KAREN sits on the arm of the sofa next to MIKE. KAREN and MIKE drink beer.

KAREN: That were nice, I thought. Wont it love?

CHARLIE: Yeah, it were pretty. Them birds were pretty.

KAREN: And all the white. It were really…delicate.

MIKE: We did her proud.

KAREN: Yeah, I think so.

MIKE: Even Princess Di didn't have a piper.

MIKE starts to cry.

CHARLIE hugs him and cries too.

KAREN puts her hand on MIKE's back.

Scene 17

The Inquiry.

CAROLINE: Cases of nvCJD continue to increase year on year, although this may be partly the result of improved detection now that my unit is being funded properly. A diagnostic test which would allow identification of the disease before brain cell damage has occurred is not yet available and treatments continue to be experimental. Dr Alan Andrews and Dr Jack Liebermann have had initial success with pentosan polysulphate, administered directly to the cerebrospinal fluid in the brain through a pump which is surgically implanted under the skin. However it will be a number of years before this treatment is available to patients.

CHAIR: The Inquiry finds that government statements to the public about BSE were misleading, played down the implications for human health and sought to give false assurance in terms that could not be justified. Important information was not made available within government departments, let alone to the public. It was this culture of secrecy that led to the fatal eleven-year delay in ministers revealing that there was a risk to human health from BSE. The government placed too much emphasis on protecting its own image and on the commercial interests of business when its over-riding concern should have been food safety.

CHAIR turns to CAROLINE and speaks informally.

Small-minded, lying little toe rags. Thank God we've finally got rid of them.

CAROLINE: 'Things can only get better.'

Scene 18

MIKE's house: MIKE and KAREN. Music: a mix tape of BECKY's songs. They clink glasses.

KAREN: Happy Birthday Becky.

MIKE: Eighteen today.

KAREN: This is the one she liked.

They sing along to 'Missing'.

KAREN: Give us a fag.

MIKE: You sure? You fallen off the wagon?

KAREN: Just tonight.

MIKE: And now you're pissing off and leaving me an' all.

KAREN: It's just a holiday Mike. I'll bring you back one of them videos you were too shy to buy yourself.

MIKE: God, we had a laugh, me and Becks, in New York. She could still have a laugh then you know. It's great there. You'll love it. Still don't know why you don't wanna take me with you, but…

KAREN: You reckon Alan wants to see you again Mike?

MIKE: Oh hey, I apologised.

KAREN: Yeah, I know. 'Sorry I punched you in the face and scared the shit out of you mate. I just needed some quinacrine.' You're a bleeding lunatic Mike.

MIKE: Yeah. Well it were all a bit…emotional. Got away with it though din't I? Thanks to that bimbo reporter police still think it were a government conspiracy. Got you your tape to give to the papers. Alan went and hooked up with Jack. You're running your nvCJD support group and that. Just me left here with nowt…

KAREN: Mike.

Let's see them photos.

They look at photos.

Oh God, that's your old Capri. That were when Debbie…

MIKE: I think our Becky were conceived in that car.

I'd love to have been a grandad.

KAREN: Still will be Mike.

MIKE: Nah.

KAREN: Our Charlie…

MIKE: Yeah, but we used to talk about it, me and Becks.

KAREN: She were great with Charlie.

MIKE: Yeah. Used to fill her head with rubbish though. Dad, don't sit there, can't you see the ghost of nan's cat? Dad can I have your toenail clippings so I can grow an alien? She'd get the poor lamb all confused. Once Charlie came to me in floods of tears cause she thought we'd eaten her Mam for dinner, cause Becky told her if you get hiccups when you're eating that's a dead person talking to you. I started shouting at Becky, calling her irresponsible, and she pretended she had really bad hiccups and then she said Debbie were talking to her and telling her I was a wanker. She said it just like Debbie would've done an all. So then I laughed me fucking head off.

KAREN: She always made you laugh.

MIKE: Yeah. Her and her Mam. I've had to bury them both. Waste of fucking time, int it?

She puts her hand on his arm.

Take no notice, it's the drink talking.

KAREN: Want another one?

MIKE: Yeah.

KAREN goes to get drinks. As soon as she's away from MIKE she cries.

MIKE looks at the photos. 'Strong Enough' plays.

You always say to people she were lovely but they don't know, you've got the photos and the videos and that but they don't know.

Here, come and look at this one.

Looks up and sees she isn't there.

Oh.

MIKE flicks through the photo album.

Scene 19

MIKE's comedy routine. MIKE remains sitting on the sofa looking at photos. Looks up and sees the audience.

MIKE: Sorry ladies and gentlemen, I'm a bit of a mess. I were just in the dressing room and there was a knock on the door. I opened it and this eight foot cockroach was stood there with a baseball bat. It beat the fuck out of me. I was saved by theatre security. They called the doctor. I explained what had happened and he said, 'Oh yeah, I've heard there's a nasty bug going round.'

I've spent the last couple of weeks talking to politicians and lawyers about compensation. What a fucking miserable shower of cunts. I offered to tell a couple of jokes about blondes to lighten things up. This fucking secretary with a telegraph pole up her arse said, 'I'm sorry Mr Chapman, I know you must be under a certain amount of pressure after the unfortunate loss of your daughter…' The unfortunate loss of my daughter, what the fuck?! She made Becky sound like the TV remote control. Anyone seen me daughter? I popped her down here but now she's gone, can't think what I did with her. This fucking woman carried on '…but I happen to be a blonde, my colleague from Liar, Bastard and Tightfist is also a blonde, as is the Minister for Agriculture. We are also all women. I think to tell jokes about blonde women would hardly be appropriate now would it?' I said 'No, not if I have to explain them three times.'

Ask yourselves, if you saw a lawyer and politician drowning and you could only save one of them would you make a cup of tea or read the fucking paper?

We went to New York. They filled our Becky full of drugs and she went yellow like a canary. Why couldn't it have been me, eh? It wouldn't of made much difference, I 'ant got much brains anyway.

I saw her first five steps and her last five.

Me daughter died. It's a sad and sorry story and every time I tell it, the end's the fucking same.

The story were all about me. Wish it had been about her.

I'm sorry, you came for stand-up and I'm sitting down.

She were so bright, beautiful, funny. Just like her Mam. I wish you'd've met her.

I'm sure if you ask at the door they'll give you your money back.

Music: 'Ain't No Sunshine'.

The End.

Printed in the USA
CPSIA information can be obtained
at www.ICGtesting.com
LVHW020853171024
794056LV00002B/516